Love's Testimony: Lost History

By: Jaired Blaine

Edited: J.W.

Scriptor House LLC

2810 N Church St Wilmington, Delaware, 19802

www.scriptorhouse.com

Phone: +1302-205-2043

Published by Scriptor House LLC

Paperback ISBN: 979-8-88692-133-5

eBook ISBN: 979-8-88692-134-2

Contents

Prelude. --iii

Part One:

The Beginning of the Found Entries. ------------------------------ 1

Part Two:

Writings throughout History --------------------------------------- 63

Chapter Three:

New World Writings--- 79

Part Four:

Our Missing Writings To Her: Our
Journals of the Old World -- 111

Epilogue: The End. ---133

Beginning of a New Chapter

Prelude.

Fourth dimension. Is love that? Is our 'other half' truly a thing? If so, it's real and we are truly stuck in some kind of simulation, a love twisted story. Things stuck and the past forgotten; old hate sparks when I see her. We all should be interconnected. We all should be as one. Interlocked to the circumference of the disturbed humanity. Being locked together as true hearts guided to one another. Calculated to the guts it takes to tell you this. My boldness stretches far beyond limits that overtake destiny. This structure is so random that I cannot begin to approach our relationship tandem. Unfortunately like this piece, abstract is all that we seem to be. Soft and gentle, your arms embrace me. They envelop me in a loving embrace. Every day I fall for you all over again. When you are not here next to me, I miss your playful retort on my skillful mind. You occupy my thoughts all day and night. I even see you in my dreams, when I drift slowly to sleep.

Some days I could break down in your arms, and there, you hold me strong. You allow me to blossom alongside you. Growing together I would do anything for you. Oh witches' lust. Leave me be with my one and only angel; flower; beautiful woman; the only person I care to know and allow my life to be motivated by my position, glory, and success. Where could we be in ten years? I don't want to waste career opportunities and wake up old and wrinkly. You make me strive for greatness even in my most draining hour. You are my sanctuary and my boldness. This piece as random and different with obscure rhyme schemes speaks for love's intents. For it is something never too random, yet, it seems like it is only of complete randomness that we are supposed to be in love with people we choose. Although love is something we may be able to choose and control, it still defies all based knowledge.

Heat at its base seems to be more random than love itself. Heat is unpredictable, always contrasting and converting energy, yet love is something even more at odds. Love can be and is everything we want it to be. Hate, joy, sadness, even desperation. Love hides in every aspect of our life; even the things and the people we despise the most; love has its traces in these. This piece, this love piece, is a declaration for what is in our hearts and what we are too scared to admit to our loved ones and to ourselves. This is a demand to be heard by all of those who have not been heard. This is an opportunity to tell the people we truly desire and love; to know we do feel such a powerful emotion for them. This piece is a piece which takes place through eternity for this is what love is; a fragile, delicate emotion that allows us to feel something so powerful that not only defines our minds but influences our actions. Love is an interstellar effect that dictates our daily standards. Love is eternal. Love is everything.

My muse, this piece is dedicated to you. No names, no fancy worship techniques. Just you, only my love for you. The others were just lust condemning my righteous soul to every hell known to exist. You have dug me up and made me anew. Our love has baffled ancient and modern times. Vaporizing our mesmerized lines, we have changed the course of relationships everywhere. My muse, my love, my flower; sing to me across our pathways of endeavors. For when I am stuck, you are the one to come to mind, to untangle all of my problems. This story will unlock new declarations of love and encourage love to be filled with desire and passion. This journalized story is how our love grew from ancient Egypt to the futuristic day. One day I might tell you, or you may know, but you will always be the only one in my heart. Every time your name comes it races and my face flushes. This piece is only for my muse and set aside for my love to her and her love to me. The epic love story.

Part One:
The Beginning of the
Found Entries.

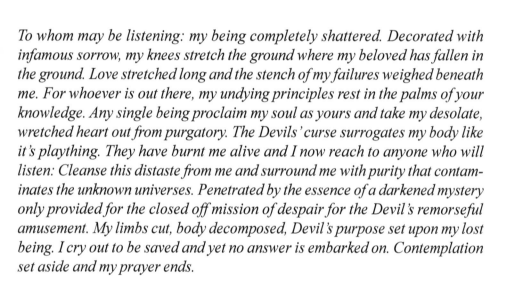

To whom may be listening: my being completely shattered. Decorated with infamous sorrow, my knees stretch the ground where my beloved has fallen in the ground. Love stretched long and the stench of my failures weighed beneath me. For whoever is out there, my undying principles rest in the palms of your knowledge. Any single being proclaim my soul as yours and take my desolate, wretched heart out from purgatory. The Devils' curse surrogates my body like it's plaything. They have burnt me alive and I now reach to anyone who will listen: Cleanse this distaste from me and surround me with purity that contaminates the unknown universes. Penetrated by the essence of a darkened mystery only provided for the closed off mission of despair for the Devil's remorseful amusement. My limbs cut, body decomposed, Devil's purpose set upon my lost being. I cry out to be saved and yet no answer is embarked on. Contemplation set aside and my prayer ends.

This lush Egyptian greenery sets upon my young,
Shattered life. My soul spreads across like sand
Sustaining any memory I had left of the glass, which
Covered the rich forests. My home is made upon
This land of treachery. My unloveable soul ruins
My emotions and these tears stain my eyes.
Can anybody guard whatever good is left?

Is all I have the puppet of my master in Hell?
Can no one hear me or is it that impossible
To save this glass departed soul? My mastered
Being is only given to the arts and this is
Only owned by him. He made my glass stained
Heart black and the knife is stuck through me.
My lust for these tails of long and engaged

Characters ruin my attempts for peace.
This memorable tail lasted as long as you lit
It, keeping it warm. Now, as I look back I wish
I let you fall apart. My desperate engagements
Stench my true heart. As the dark collected, my
Shadow falls upon the ground in desperate measure;
I couldn't run fast enough to disappear into this world

Maintaining myself as a dominant figure.
My delicate nature giving in to a source
Of stability. My soul now a depressed
Character of my former self. Concentration
No longer suits the being, controlling
Every movement my secular being
Tries making. These thoughts pertaining

To a maneuvering effort to break these aching
Similarities between my own characters and myself.
I cannot seem to gain any prospect of my own life.
I glance at the sky as thunder crackles and lightning
Breaks the sky. The clouds turn red and as the rain
Fell to the ground, it too turned red. I opened my mouth
To gain insight on this unique change. To my surprise

It tasted like blood. Confused I cock my head to the sky
And chunks of rock fell through. People fall from the
Opening crack as well. Is this world coming to an end?
All of a sudden the sky cleared up and a green floating
Object headed my way.

I heard your prayer, the mysterious voice echoed from the air itself.

Who is it I may be listening to?

*Osiris. The green God of fertility. I have defeated my siblings, and you
now will do my bidding and serve me loyally on this plane.*

Confusion set upon my thoughts
I slightly bow to show understanding.
The creature suddenly disappeared
Back into the clouds where he appeared.
All at once hundreds of thoughts and rules
Entered my head. Seems like I haven't actually
Learned anything with my bout with the Devil.

I can never fall into love, well at least
Something will be easy to accomplish.

Seems like I am unlovable anyways.
Not having a relationship will allow
My focus to center on the greater tales anyways.
Easily, I will be able to accomplish something
As remote as this task.

The second thing devouring my mind
Is to spread his victories and worship
Throughout the lands. This easily begins
To take form for my popularity already
Stretches this mighty state.
These two things were clearly the most important
And to say my heart no longer exists

And my popularity of tales; Osiris
Will be the biggest known name to date.
The God of Fertility. Does this mean youth
And lush fields? This makes it
Even more easy. My great Osiris, I shall
Forever serve you as the greatest
God of this mighty empire.

Though, what if your siblings get jealous
And kill me? These risks were very
Necessary risks for me. I shall do you
Wonders Osiris. My thoughts turn to him.
Maybe a slight setback, but I have nothing
To hide anyways. He has freed my soul from
The dictating master of the underworld.

I can do this with ease.
This world, shaped upon my feet,
Delicate to those above and below.

She lay beneath me in this hollow,
Yet sacred ground. He came on the
Day her burial was.

He knows in grief anything is accepted
And my heart betrayed me yet again.
For as promises stench the late

Mildew air, lies overshadow the deepened
Darkened night. Heart slumped upon my chest
And the slight tears flounder in my eye.

Lost and only found by my crying out,
Undisciplined in nature I continuously
Stretch the incomplete glass heart.

Dust grabbed at the ground as my tears turn
The ground to mud as glass turns to dust.
A majestic way the world turns.

Solemnly I walk back to my home
Where I left my real heart, under the knife,
When you put it through my back.

My heart stretched to the ceiling and
Lies split the air in the middle leading
To considerably wretched territory.

Condemned to prosperity I cannot reach;

You're being lacerates my comparing intelligence.

Only containing enough for the first act.

Is this how you are going to serve me! Osiris thundered through my ceiling. *You start serving me with discipline and convenience. Prosperity only serves those demanding it. This sobbing and darkened position you sustain yourself is disgusting. I will not play pompous to a saddened, condemned boy. This dedication to love is in the grave. You must move on with care and grace and this is not doing it. How must you move on out there without this disheartening throw?*

Your rule was to never truly love.

This is gross. You may love if dedication systematically is shared; philosophy and your weak human tendencies; but true love, no. This slipping further and further will show you to your grave early. Go out there and celebrate this life. You only get one. With this the house fell silent.

My liability is shamed into this raining world. One of pleasure, greenery and lust. He has provided delicate care and I shall give this back. These days pass long and hard and yet no one has listened to me. For days upon hours upon the sand walls of this kingdom, everyone turns their ears. Dehydration settled upon my skin and you peered into the sand. Sadness stretched, my feet stepped in front of each other as I whispered the dedication Osiris has granted me to the world. You stepped out of this lust filled dust towards the greenery which has started from his gift to this world. His growth has only been settled upon my hands and his thanks is to grant me a love shared through history and arch. My hand lifted to her shoulder and she jumped in startled perplexity. I admired her gracious light emerald eyes. Her smiles turned outwards when she saw my lips whispering the words of Osiris. Water was granted and true purity flowed flawlessly through my veins. Months gone by since my last conversation with my love and here she is, reincarnated. The delicate creature stood in front of me and as I spoke she instantly caught into flames.

You fool. You thought you could betray me? I am the King, the God, the Healer and the Giver. You cannot trick my being, for your thoughts are mine.

You said I could—

I said no such thing, you coward. Now work and work properly. Inspiration and our connection is counting on it. For if I shall perish and so shall you.

Nights giving way to forever lustful
Inspiration. Osiris knocking in my mind,
Yet this entire land now is filled with greenery

Simply for my delicate sword of a tongue.
Confidence soaring through the lasting air
And I have yet to find a way to block you out of my mind.

I feel you wiggle and twirl; trying to set myself free,
I cannot be so desperately invasive of this invading
Presence of yours. You try and stabilize and so

I refuse to allow my mind a break. When I do, your
Strength swallows my dedication. Normalcy has left
My life and only can I stand here to teach

My cowardice is a lesson in life.
No longer the sad boy you have met.
Over ten years of growth, twenty five blesses me.

Nobody is marrying me off to anybody anymore.
I have made the decision to replace you furthermore.
I slowly hide away these thoughts to seek out the witch

To batter together something to barricade you
Out of my mind. This headache you give me will be reduced
When I find her. The journey long and you start

To question where I am going, yet you cannot
Harm me without harming you, so the trip we both
Are on. The hours long and I have traveled

11

For days and I believe her cave is in front of me.
I can hear you question what this was.
I walked in and she immediately put a trap around me.

She glared at me and knew what I came for.
Soon she started telling me what she had done.
She warned me to be careful since it might not

Be permanent. Though, at least for now, I've fought
My fight and for the first time in awhile the voices
Quiet and gone. Mind is no longer tattered.

My walk back had my own mind wandering.
All I must do is stay alive long enough to shatter
Your own mentality. Ten times the effort I induce sustaining the wall.

Now my morning insists walks through the lasting lush
Greenery of my home in the great Egyptian
World. My mind stabilizes with each mornings blush,

Conditioning my preserved soul into one corrected being.
My lonely hearts desire entrapts my love for Osiris
For my heart cannot know any others love; for being

Alone is my sufferable cause for only
Other than my God Osiris. I shall forever hold this
Curse upon my restrained head.

As the lush grass rises forward I see you ahead in the distance.
I immediately fell in love with you. Your hair, curly and your darkened,
Tan skin glowed, basking in the sun. Your eyes resisting

The torment of the early Egyptian empire. Sparkling in the far outreach,
Her dress glowed in the early morning breeze. I must find out who she is;
Where she came from; where does she hail from? Her mind breaches

And no longer am I able to harmonize into one central being.
My soul urns to be with you forever, yet I have only seen you.
Seems I have been falsifying my feelings

Having them only for Osiris has made me suffer completely.
Though I cannot hope to ruin such characters of Egypt
For a love which may not even exist yet. I must have to be free

Of these emotions; for this greenery cannot be turned into
A desert wasteland, for this shall turn the tide of empires.
Merciless love cannot give way destroying this blissful power.

You took my breath away stealing my minds dignity from
Myself and the great, green God Osiris. My friend sustains this
Lush planet as I maintain to real the beliefs in for him.

His rule only works as I can maintain belief in only him,
For he has been a jealous God. My mind centers again
On Osiris, yet as the end of this solitude walk

Continues, you stretch back into my mind.
He decorates you with misfortune and blasphemy.
Every time you start to slowly drift into my

Mind, he cuts you out with distractions bland
And eagerness showing depth and prospect
Illuminating upon your gentle flesh.

13

He comes through as bushes and the moon
Speaks from his voice. He lights my soul
To fire, ensuring my being does not waiver.

Unconsciously I begin to lose judgment
And he takes control. With himself in mind
Over my body, he fuels these peoples minds.

The Egyptian world expanded, and as they did,
So did he. He shouted from the rooftops of the
Blessings and promises I witnessed and yet,

It is in my being he lied, stole and diminished
The aching my being is truly feeling. If I don't
Participate though, he has threatened to kill

You; you are with me in the passenger seat.
Casting the shroud I begin to melt into
The one I was, when I was with him.

Soon, you no longer exist to half of me.
Silent accord was what you are to me now.
He put an alert in my subconscious mind

Hanging you like a Christmas tree,
Alerting me of his steady monitoring
Of my being and my mind.

My drunken, mystic eyes, first fell
For your gorgeous life.
I must see your decorated,

Stunning eyes, as soon as possible.

Life passes and yet, I am the only

One who is responsible, willing, seeing through them;

To see your beauty.

How could God not put my radar

In absolutely everybody.

They could see what I do.

Your skin, gentle, soft, milky.

Lighter than the stardust which

Falls in my hand late at night.

I miss your presence when you are too far away,

And your voice when I cannot hear you speak.

My ears and mind are in your care and soon,

When we trust and open up to each other, we can

Fully give each other our hearts and souls.

My mind is already out there for you to take,

One day I hope you lock it away.

My life can be expanded to yours, I try to relate

My feelings with you and I feel more deeply

Than anybody else. My heart, soul, and emotions

Have no end. An endless, bottomless pit, they continue

To travel and travel like my infinite love to you.

Maturity grows and determination settles upon

A thought which dissipates into this love I

Will share with you one day.

I fear if I enter a relationship,
I would be stuck and trapped, enclosed
Into a tightly knit life that I'll enjoy. These fears are outshined

By beauty and intuition. Echoing in my heart
I do want to be with you. Constellations
Of my life and your eyes allow me to see worlds wide.

My vulnerability and love is overwhelming at points.
Feeling this deeply causes roots of transparency
We have not seen before.

Emotions are different as I foresee them.
Written words woe on my longed mind
I see now, for you, they continue to

Deepen as the strategic plan races a charismatic
Syringe forcing itself into my skin. Chaotic carnage
Stages my darkest desires and the moisture

From lotion soaks in me like my love and passion,
Yet where it's supposed to stop, it doesn't, it runs like
A river meeting a waterfall. Vigorous and never ending,

Moisture getting soaked up through the sun and then
Rain spreads my love and passion everywhere. An unsettled
Ancient life of water which my feelings have never ceased.

I know out of all this you may think of me as
Obsessing, maybe I am, but, I am completely passionate
About you and everything you challenge me to.

You look like me, rare to find, oh, might I say
Your love from afar is a gracious technique.
Understanding my short phrases you inherit
My power of understandment. How I can relish
Holding you to the nights candle, engaging prosperity
In a future where without Osiris we could be a full mind.
My thoughts could be yours, but if he is destroyed,
So am I.

I cannot seem to be more blunt, yet I cannot
Get you out of my mind. I have dreamt of you
Constantly. Maybe too suddenly, but would

You want to elope with me?
Even now I can feel him wiggle, trying to set himself free.
Being more careful of my thoughts like the beginning.
My mind playing a trick on me when I first laid my eyes upon you.
Your dress enveloped your color, your eyes couldn't be

More heavenly matched.
How can I continue to feel intensely for
Hundreds of different people simultaneously?
I need her to sweep me from my knees
And if I stay in her way she could do it for me,

Truly, you are the perfect one for me.
Your lips slightly parted and smiled at me before her eyes twinkled at me.
The beauty seeped out of your dress
Following down to your legs and feet.

17

This beauty you portray sings to my heart
Decorating my soul from further despair
And agony. I try to talk to you every day after.

Would you be with me?
Can you take me for the rest of your life?
Could we start a family together?

Is this my psyche inside of me telling me what to do and say?
Will you still like me if I am crazy and full of psychotic love?
I vow to be your one and only love.

The vows I have written in my head for you
Are the ones which I have declared to be only
The most insatiable of love to you.

You are my Syringa. My beautiful flower which
Blossoms into a gorgeous delicate creature.
Roots are strong, my being forever yours

Rescue and parade my new soul. The words I swallow are the
Ones I know I must ask you. Every glance
You run away with. What if instead we ran

To explore the world?
We have a long way to go, maybe something will happen.
My heart, your heart, is it one contraption?

How can I be a man when I open up to you?
My fears and my loves you begin to know,
Now is where I ask you

I know it's too early, maybe this is my obsession?
After all the great Osiris doesn't appreciate
Anything other than the worship of him.

After I saw you lead back to your house
I memorized where I needed to deliver my messages
To you. Afterwards I went straight to the market

And picked up a delivery bird.
Sleek black feathers glistened in
Early morning sun. I stuck the letter

To him and showed him where to go.
I watched him fly throughout the wind,
Flapping graciously throughout the sky.

I saw him fly to your window and he dropped
The letter in your hands. You peered out,
Looked around, then opened it.

To your heart,

Miss, I have seen you these past few mornings and you have not noticed me. For every time I catch a glimpse of your eyes shining from the beauty of the sun, you have turned and you have run. My heart has been attached to you in the awe inspired movements of your essence. Your beauty cannot be described for I am a teller and poet and yet it seems the only thing I can describe is the radiancy the sun drops from you as if you made Venus and Aphrodite. Angels seem to blush as the sun drops and rises throughout the day, surrounding you. It is only I who has seen the images of the sky become jealous of your presence. Intelligence and dedication drapes from you as the great philosophers ache to join you in unison. Treasures stimulate and appear from out of nowhere. Even the steps you take upon this blessed formulates the softest touch, embracing your impact as if you were too delicate to allow a misstep. My dear love, I wish this reaches you in your truest form. You have stimulated my mind far past anything before. Be my perfection and we shall be in love forever.

Your Truest,
Morning Grace

During these noted conversations, you explained
I was the only one nice to you?
You deserve the world; you continuously make me a better specimen.

You're the first person I want to fully know and to fully know me.
My dedication to Osiris makes me see I can be dedicated to you,
Now through many anew.

Do you know why?
Please don't be afraid to trust in a leap of faith.
My red wine truly ends up drained.

Our first day together will drain our lives stories.
My daydreaming cut short as a visit with Osiris cut my mind.
Warnings not of celleby rang from his tongue of a desert to be.

Thoughts go back to her though.
Why must love be a thought,
Stuck in my mind, like a boat with holes having to quickly row

To make it back to land in safe measure.
My thoughts of you, unfortunately, are not disappearing.
I never want your eyes filled with tears and yet,

I do not know how to completely make this happen,
For I cannot talk to you. Every time our glances catch
You run the opposite way. I wish I could tell you I love you.

What if I gave you all of me? Trusted you with everything?
Sex should be an art and yet people buy for fake comprehensions.
This would be something I gave you, risking everything.

Osiris, my green God, makes me a God with continued being.

If we ever have something other than this dream let's celebrate it.
I allow Osiris to lie to me, but yet, what if he is telling the truth?

What would you do with that power?
I see myself as a God. I could give you your own world.
Should I say babe? Should I keep this loosely based

Love song?
I don't know what I could say and release from our encased
Short story.

Now a deer sweet bird
With two red stripes on
Both wings lands on my

Window seal. I reach out, palm open,
A small letter falls into my hand.
It has **To: Morning Grace**

Written upon its seal.
She must have followed
Me to my study when

I wasn't paying any attention.
This ordeal Osiris traps me in,
Doesn't allot for many fully sought

After thoughts of anything other than him.
I alter my mind trying to barricade
Him out it, just long enough to read.

To: Morning Grace,

 I have received your letter with grace. Prosperity has filled my ears and her complexity filled my eternal soul. Such delicate ease prospers in the sound of your voice in my head as I read it. I too have seen and noticed our glances, awkward in tone, yet as they hit me I get flattered. Your jawline cut sharp and your charisma seeps through your delicate being. Sadness

Drifts from your eyes like the ice in sweltering heat. Intellect you write with spills me over the

Edge, falling deeply for the intensity of a distinctful relationship. Mattering only to the physiology

The aching of missing your presence this morning seeps from my thoughts and onto the languid

Afternoon you delicately describe. These earthly beings competence overarch the principles of

True love and enduring thoughts.

 Complexities wrestle grave circumferences and dance in the

Aching in the multitudes of these galaxies. The Gods have to stretch down and learn from your

Charisma and pure complex and intelligent thoughts. A labrinth stretches forever and so to does

Your mastered self controlled destiny. Future seen but unclear, yet I have noticed only you

Stretching for intensity that has already been decaying in so many minds. This peace and chivalry

Stench the homeland of this great country, for war has brought it to an end. My dear love,

Our madness will stretch galaxies and our love to primitive to gather in small detail. One day we

Shall set forward in each other's lives and consist solely for each other's being. My simply lit soul

Burns for passion my foresight has blessed me with.

        Truly One Day Yoursss,
           My purest heart

Oh dear love, how the stars have aligned,
Oh magnificent being, take your love to my soul.
My now lifeless soul seeks you.
Longing for recollection of your arms in mine.
How feelings approached me and yet
It seems to only be me reciprocating these feelings.

It seems only yesterday our hearts aligned.
Now the days go by, when my heart cries
Out to talk to you, even a soft hi to appease my ears.
Desperate, I seek to love you,
For how could something so powerful
Not even get the chance to see what it could be for our souls.

How could we not owe each other this?
Are you scared to see where it may go?
For the fright in me does not coexist
With the love that forever touches me.

When I got your message
The other day;
My heart stumbled
Over beats too many to count
And ceased to be.

My Morning Delight,
These glances hidden only to my sight.
Too many could become dangerous to outsiders.
I do however share feelings mutual to yours.

Blood refilled my cold forgotten body
Showering my eternal soul into an endeavor
Hunger to be with you.

The search for my eternal one;
Has stalled by the stench of my darkened soul;
For the trueness of white deepening in my heart.

Pure white and dark; soul aching
For yours to be tightened into mine.
Just like a hook in a fishes mouth
Reeling into my net of love.

For if you were mine, love
Would scour the world,
Brightening everything in our wake.
Spreading eternal grace in our steps.

My heart has exploded with anguish,
Yet my eyes are blind from laughter.
Tears pass my hands as they fill
With the salty sweat of nervousness.

I am in utter love.

Her eyes strike like the tidal waves with
Her perfect accent.
Her hair, oh her hair.

I could listen to you all day,
But, unfortunately, your heart
Calls you back to your home.

I leave a piece of my heart with you.

No matter the beauty of the world's creations, I seem to never
Get you out of my mind. Heart fluttering, heavenly,
To someone who aches my heart to meet, longing
To take her hand and share one dance or song
With her and let her feel the peace she brings
To every occurance of my heart's leap.
Even the sadness in your tone while
You perfect the double meanings.
I would never just want to be a fling,
But even that is better than the lowest seeping
Pit my heart can achieve while filing
Your name in my mind in ongoing suspense to marry you, seemingly
The only name that would ever be in such a category.

For you, my only true companion,
Stitched and scarred my heart,
But you make life this crazy gamble.
Osiris trying to bury inside my mind sacrificing
My life's loves who have been buried for eternity.

How can I give Osiris up when this threat
Could be true. I need to talk to you.
This love   lust   love, needs to be declared.

Where is the future if we're not building today?
Osiris, how can this be true? WIll you grant me
One mistake? Can this even be a mistake?
I am putting everyone at risk for something which
May not even be
Something. Could this be fake?
Is there something I have missed?
How can you risk everything to prove your point?
If she dies, why would I help you?

Then the ringing started again, and I could feel the blockade start to crumble.
I would poison her. Only then will you help, for I would have the cure.

Now delicate to my situation I leave my study getting a fresh breath of air.

As I finally catch up to you
On your way again running from sight.
When I touched your arm for the first time,
Your skin is too soft to touch. When seeing your
Eyes deepened, I knew from there I was in a bind.
My words straddled the back of my throat as
Every time I tried to speak they gripped tighter,
Unable for myself to breathe as my words barely give way.
Your eyes sparkle off the tint of midday sun.
Every second I begin to speak they entrap my entity.
Tight and suffocating the labyrinth my mind has set in

Has everything on hold. You turn away and this is when I grab you.

I proclaim the meaning of my feelings and urge you to disappear

From my mind, fearing you would be dead from Osiris.

I urge you and try to explain his threats.

You nodded like you heard, yet you give me the look

You give when you are about to do something we know

You shouldn't do. Oh syringa don't.

I don't know how these things are done. I've never been able

To converse with anyone. Well anyone but him.

The big guy. The guy in the sky who only talks to me. Osiris.

My one and true mission.

The one who threatened to turn our dearest homeland

To complete desert sand

If I do not comply with his demands.

I never thought I could love again.

It simply never spoke to me.

Darkness gathered my heart; no one's light

Could ever shine through to my mystified

Being. Soul paraded with blood

And I still stand side-by-side in harmony

To you. My dearest one. My beautiful syringa.

The one turned my love to only him;

And yet, it is you who breaks the spell the magician has me in.

This powerful God treated me like his son and condemns me only

To be his, to only talk to him, to only be with him.

You though, you are grace,

You are imperfect perfection.

You're what love has inspired to be.

You're the love of my everything.

Was coming out boldly a mistake?

My eyes have yet to dilate.

Confidence soars, annihilating

My weak feelings, begin to frustrate

This structure falls apart.

I need a restart, a jumpstart,

Getting to one point to another

Quickly, swiftly, always pondering.

Red, black, races across my eyes.

Lightning glares past me endangering my being.

I beg, stay in my dreams

Just for this night.

Numbness of my old life triggers.

Light hits your leather, catching my eyes.

Your eyes. Oh those eyes.

Lightly stained gray as blue sparks try

Raining from them like meteor showers.

Every day a unique comet crosses them;

Lighting up every dulled room.

My inspiration;

You blossom as people tear you into

The earth, but I know flowers

Bloom when placed in the ground.

No one is more sustaining of a more

Glimmerous beam of your fiery passion

Which lights your contraction. You

Work every day to chase your ideas.

To make a tortured artist brightly covered

In blushed cheeks and a hazed smile.

On the other side of your beauty,
Sadness tries to leap from your half blushed smile.
If anything is off, tell me.
I can be your safety. Your embassy.
Intertwining our lives fuller.
I beg, but don't know how to tell you
Maybe these feelings have grown.
I say love because
I know that's the truth.
I'll never lie to you.
Forgive me if I am too straightforward.
Releasing to the public after a glance.

This confidence I enclose now is completely
different than the ones I show you.
How bold am I allowed to be Osiris?
Is a look even too much to ask for?
All this difference is eating at me.
This confidence penetrates me.
If I could see. If only you could see.
Don't tell me it's too late to be.

For as our conversation lingers
Your voice and structure give way
To signs of a dying heart desperate
To be with you.

I wish I got a redo as the poison drips from you,
I would ask Osiris if he would allow it.
Flowers, dinner, night under the stars.
What would you have said?

Your admiration, mystical presence.

Could you be a brilliant witch?

Casting a love spell on me.

How I cannot stop thinking about you.

Osiris grows, inspiring the world, he shines through me,

He shines lighter in the world,

He clearly does not need me.

He cannot need my belief or power anymore.

Granted I never thought I would love again, but here we are.

But lately I got to tell you.

So I dare question again,

Can I just have a small conversation?

Their reserved for love,

You, us, we feel right.

These days the only way to communicate

Is when my love is professed to those

Watching over you, but I could take you.

For again, love is my heart to you.

What's different?

I ponder, but my thoughts

Come to you yet again.

Born again, life inspired, regained.

The old greats influenced me;

And you, as my muse, puts me

Into a trance where

All this is for my heart, telling you

I am completely in love with you.

I read your soul as you try to read my mind;
And it is because these great writers
You can be my muse. My career hasn't
Been fruitful and yet it is because
I haven't had this steady muse
Until I discovered you.

Flying away like birds,
Yet here I am grounded
To the floor like nails on a cross,
Not bounded, but,
Alongways tossed
For better operations
For the once overpowering
God.

Everything better and more complex
Verse every day friends.
Your intelligence strengthens my
Mind as when I sleep and your pictured,
I no longer need to fear the devilish
Green God. Your complexity has allowed
Me to push myself to higher mountains.
Humans, easy and predictable, so why can I not
Predict you my flower?

My coherency with you from this magnitude is nothing less than immaculacy.
Just like the tremendous flower you come from, blossoming
Through the world next to Canopic
Creek. Our doors open, rotating.
Although it'd be nice if they shut; contemplating

Such a beautiful time we'd have with
The prime of adventures under our belts.

My walk through this garden reminds me of our first meeting.
At the time Osiris was in complete control of my mind.
The nice thing is I was able to spread the word so well,
I no longer have to spread the word.

You thought you could trap me forever. When I get out and I will,
You will pay for this. I don't care if I get hurt back, you will
Pay for this terrorist act. You will not condemn me, and I will-

He cut out and my breathe no longer
In my chest. Discipline was lack and further
Slips my slacked being. He always told
His plan for me. He always reminded me of his power.
Who do I think I am? Love crazed has me blistering in pain.

Osiris speaks of great worlds which needs adventures,
But he won't leave until everyone, like me, has his support.
Back to you my mind goes. Every inch of you is angelic.
Like a poem, beauty is shown in nature.
You stand tall in regard to nature. Simultaneously barbaric,
Everyone around you on tenure.

No one could come close
To you. How I could all day boast
About you and your impactable intelligence.
Beauty impeccable. We fit like a ratchet

To its socket. What makes you special?
I think it's simple.
My soul longs for the intellectual conversations
And a soul similar in comparison.

I think it's too simple.
Anything about us you can compare,
Nothing can electrify our special
Connection when we are in conversation.

Your description is like the syringa.
Your seed always blooming,
As elegantly as words allow me to bill.
Pushing him back these words allow me to fill
Our every day extravagant relationship;
Which seeps into my mind like Osiris'
Mighty spell has me rippling
Through all kinds of different feelings.
Fears allow my strength to be bold ripping
Everything not Osiris out, but you, a virus
Holding me in one cage,
Alerting him of the world's fractured support.
People celebrating his leadership, yet no one
Could possibly know him besides me.

People around me crippled
By their fears, yet, I have the angel
Of my dreams; and the God in me

Is trying to escape.
Your beauty is one thing

That allows every elegant thought

Escape my mind

Onto this bleaked white paper

Since I cannot talk to you, or share my thoughts to you;

I write on a soft paper and set it on fire so Osiris won't

Know of any wavering thoughts setting back his lush rule.

These sentences bare weight of my heart,

But if he shows himself as my family he can enter

My house. He shows himself as beings

That are close to me to where I no longer have a family,

If I did he would become them. His eyes enlarge

Near my house, hoping I mess up so he can burn you too.

If he is my only family,

How will I be able to be with you?

Should we run and elope?

Would he find us elsewhere?

You are my constant thought,

The thing allowing my sanity

To extend higher

Then my confidence to envelop with you now.

They're dour faces stretch from my mind, yet I am too busy

With holding him to be stuck on that, especially with your purity

In my mind. Not the purity that means pure,

But this purity of your complete trinity.

Nobody can take you from me; or I from you.

My heart's delicacy will always find my way back to you.

The infamous necromancer can try to lace

Your body with poison, but none can ever be of such desperation.
Loving you completely is enough to relish your feared
Mark of jealousy. I will cover up any deaths you commit for me.

From your lips alone, soft and parted, one more kiss I exhume
Before we split ways, for our days again.
My syringa, inhale my being and be my love.

What little sliver of lust I had left, has fumed
Out of my body full of love. Eager to be
At your side since our eyes interlocked.

The urge of being there is mounted against
Everything I thought possible.
Flirting of our eyes and smiles we exchange

When we think neither one is looking, it is heart racing.
How you purify my dreams of
Blissful thoughts and memories make my heart race.

These butterflies seem to never cease, and if that is the case
You must be the right one. This vulnerability I am fighting
For you completes me. My fears and flaws I want you to know.

These fears run long and deep; but I know we will always be healthy.
When a bird lands I see your name;
A smile is comfortably set upon my face.

I knew you were the one when I continued to
Question everything I knew in life. The challenge of
Intellectual strength arose in my being,

As I leaned on you for more of a crutch to
Help me push balance and gains to a permanent
Infrastructure only you could design and have me desire.

Will today be the day where I grab hold of these feelings
Squirming inside of us, pinning them, allowing confidence
To soar? I don't know if I could allow myself to fail at this ancient

Endeavor I have dreamed about; so desperately wishing
For you to say yes. I am confident in heart you will, but if you say no
My mind is convincing, I could lose you forever. These doubts I flush

Away. Oh how I miss you now, even though your close and near,
My heart aches that we are not together. Your voice still gives
Me goosebumps, I desperately want for eternity like your gentle touch.

The peace you bring my soul is something
I wish to maintain daily. I can only dream about that solemn
Touch and grace you provide and I am hoping to be with you

Every day for eternity. My heart thumping
Inside my chest and your the
Only reason why. Forever loyal and love never on fumes,

Every time I think of you my smile grows big, my blush warm.
You are intoxicating and stunning while my anguish grows
To a prospected amount only you can subside.

The peace you bring is unmatched
And calms the locked ferocious beast straining my mind.
You make me humble and cocky all in one motion.

I could have misinterpreted your glances and awe movements.

Maybe we are better as friends because of this.

Will you hold my aggression towards unlocking my potential, or is this my

Mind cracking, put on full display.

I cannot remember these little things.

Barricade erodes any memory I wish I had, but is our

Full potential at bay? Will I wake up one day

Wishing I had made a different choice?

It really isn't a hard question.

Would you marry me?

Not hard, not complicated, but love, you are

My soul mate. My one true inspirational muse.

I just need to ask, it is not that hard.

I have these true feelings for you yet,

I struggle with this side of me. Vulnerability.

One more chance, can it be? If I ask you will you be pleased?

Stuck in the middle of my conscious and subconscious,

I cannot win a war that is going inside my head.

Time is slowly ticking away, yet you are continuously

On my mind. The power we hold together is

A force which is untouchable by any who surround us.

Just a few more minutes and I will ask you to marry me.

The cool morning air dark in mood, but love and happiness pour out of me.

My heart burns with joy as my tempered voice

Blockading Osiris, falling to my knees, grabbing your soft
Cracked hands and gently fighting back a headache
Osiris is giving me, syringa, will you protect my mind

As I shall protect your sickness he's granted you? Will you forever
Hold my being for eternity showering all those who
Stand in our paths, will you always be mine?

When the gentle words left your voice
My heart skipped a beat. The Yes, my
Ears and elegance of your charisma mesmerized my mind.

With my heart, soul and mind evenly on the same page,
I can finally move forward being with you forever.
Though, worries start to intrude the blockade in my mind.

Will you love me forever if he comes in; or will you
At least consider my hand in yours when you find the dark
Crescents my life is riddled with from past mistakes?

The one thing I will always do is never lie to you.
I could never betray you, I shall always be there.
My love for you could never falter until the Insofars fall

And the Hells rise. Knowing love exists and you are the one,
Resting easy, only dreaming of you. Your head resting easy on mine.
How my love in the morning rises and by night my love grows with my dreams.

Sunset to sunrise, sunrise to sunset, how much I love you
Until death does arise. My heart's desire and soul
Gripping Osiris from mind where you then enter, beating him back.

My being starts to fade in and out and we know now he was serious.
The connection unraveling where my already sold soul was desperately
Trying to escape his claws. My life contained to only one existence now,

As you gently maneuver his hands around the crippling
Memories which now pour into my mind of despair and worry.
When you come out telling me you succeeded, my body

Fluttering upon the floor and you know I cannot hold on.
Your hands grip tight, and strangle the tempered, anger, despair, every-
thing, but Osiris,
Sucking it into you. Your soul now blackened of my being

And when my eyes flutter you see the sadness upon my face.
You hold me, comforting and ensuring we would make it through.
You exchanged your life for mine and my fragile being

Shatters itself until I fall, blackening out.
My pure thoughts flutter around the nightmares
Slipping my delicate state. My eyes flutter and the

Morning day stings with you by my side.
Interlocked, arms in arms, how we are aware
Of our eternal love and enduring happiness.
Headache sings barely remembering the night before.

Your intelligence has proved to be barely in comparison.
Communication has been silent since my proposition.
Intelligence has been a clear factor for this is what needs to be.

Your beauty doesn't need to be told anymore.
Your eyes flutter and flirt, my heart always stutters.
Every time I talk to you, my mouth cannot utter the words I wanna say.

How your presence has healed my soul,
Calming me for all eternity.
The slightest message of yours brings me

True peace with a full smile upon my face.
Complete and utter innocence
My passion coincides with yours.

My heart full, I cannot wait until you are in my presence again.
Your lips upon mine, I feel and lust after the soft gentle feelings
They give me. Oh how my passion is fueled and

Intensity constructs the tension between us.
I bite my lip, yet, I am completely
Vulnerable and I could only show you, since Osiris kept everyone at bay,

Is more than I show anyone else around me.
Though, I am working on showing you all of me
Even when it is hard trying to show you any of me.

You think he can truly break through this blockade.
All of this is the truth and besides him you
Are the only people my mind fades to.

My heavy attraction
To you is not just physically, but spiritually and emotionally,
Every day is a new challenge opening up to you.

My dreams about you last for hours.
It's weird how when you edit past mistakes,
There are no aspirations to be without you,

Every time I see you it is something
Magical I haven't seen before. Something
Only true peace and complete bliss.

I used to think I knew peace,
But when I sit next to you, my heart
Instantly calms in your presence,

When your soft eyes look at me,
When your voice gentle, a little stressed on radar,
Beauty speaks, I no longer feel anything besides bliss.

Hope and intellectual being inspires everything.
I have been filled with the spirit and love you give.
Shared philosophies and exact beings, I am stuck

In the middle of these two beings, and both sides of me
Ache to be with someone, one side though,
Wishes to be in a nonstop working mentality.

These poems I write about you stretch and decorate the papyrus.
The page empty, yet when you come to me,
Even my mind is deceased to him. Blockade doing its job.

Now I can finally write everything I need to.
Full desires critique the mistful morning.
Full being finally out from being cornered.

A relationship with work, yet my body, cold, laying
Next to these loosely stacked papers. She though,
Warms my body. Warmth inspiration seeps through her.

Galaxies and cosmos stretch with my passions and fears.
I have never felt as much as I have felt now.
Wherever we may be;

I will always care and protect you. Over mountains and
Upon the mountains, I will be there to guide you. Us.
Your hug, my heart raced at the thought, then it slowed

When your head hit my shoulder. Suddenly peace circulated
My ever lost being.
When we are together, in arms, my soul is complete. We are real.

Your passion about life and compassion you have for others
Spread upon the universe never getting diverse or twisted,
Spinning to something different than your true vibrating self.

My genius, my beauty; you are the only specimen who can
Contain me and match my veracity. Only you.
Thousands of words soak these pages I write, though nothing yet

Has been able to describe you. I trust you completely, which is rare
On a human being case. My favorite specimen.
My only superhero. Syringa, I hope you see me the same.

The uniqueness you portray is grandeur and
The deeper we become the deeper I feel.
I'd shatter the space-time continuum for you.

I would be as selfish as I could be with you.
The minutes apart feel dull and drag on.
My honesty would always be yours and alone yours to be.

My only desire is to be with you selflessly, yet
I can't see a place where my accommodations of us
Are full and not in disarray. I want to be with you completely,

Whatever you need. I don't want to overstep
In a particular way, yet I can only see myself being me and
That is an equal part of bad and good; although I cannot

Seem to justify a love hidden and deep within me.
The harsh manipulations of past relations have
Always haunted my past being. I can put everything out there,

And yet, I take everything in. I care ultimately
For only one human being. Truly care on every scale.

My only objective is to save your life and this world
Has allowed me to do such a thing.

Osiris tried poisoning everyone with your name.
I just found out, how can I keep him fully at bay?
Should I go back to the witch? What's next though?
Do I now forget you?

You have allowed my spirit to obtain more knowledge
Than anyone else in this world has ever known.
I continue to fight for your prosperity and

This world to ensure your safety.

We never want to leave, people are pulled apart eternally.

We keep not working for the life we choose and yet

Your smile and laugh allows my heart to rejoice.

My muse keeps me going, working, to become the best.

My care, heart, and soul only are to you.

It's weird you are the one condemning me to be the best.

You have made my heart rapid and can slow it within

A few seconds. Only you can allow my heart to be paced

By your touch. Your trust. Your care and when you're near.

Compassion and passion separate meaning from bliss.

My heart blows up big and my brain and soul echo

Each other. All in unison. I want nothing more

Than to protect you and spin our lives to everything

Of hope and passion, you put into each others

Compartment of realism with each of your writings. Missing each other when we

were gone on a molecular level. I used to not be able to love anybody fully, yet I want

Nothing more to fathom the love that could spark

Between us. Pages rise then comprise into a supercharged

Love into a composed being. Loving touch caresses us into

A being of raw intensity. Whenever your close feelings bent

And broken to nothing then peace intercepts any dismay I encounter.

You integrate normalcy with perfection in a raw
Form my dreams are flourishing with you.

My Syringa,

    As the ten months after my first love's death, I never believed in what love could be. My heart ached and almost brought me to tears. This letter is hard to write, because every time I do, I end up erasing everything. She left and I was too much of a coward to tell her how I really felt. Shattered, my heart turned black and I could never have put myself out there. I didn't know at the time what I was feeling. I didn't know that this feeling of love was as powerful as it was, so I forced it deep down and never dealt with it, or even told my full feelings.

He slipped into my mind as your name started to come in and barely got it
pushed down. He found out and he tortured my being trying to locate

You and he could not do so, for I refused to let you get

Torn away from me. This condemned, trapped, and killed him.

My heart starts to get weak, but as the lush

Turned to desert, my soul pushes back in my chest.

He poisoned every woman that enjoyed the calming syringa, even them
themselves,

And your sickness continues to seep within

You, because of me. All of these deaths, because of me.

As I go back and relook, my mind must be struggling,

For I now have repeated what I have already told you.

I just need to be in your arms before this tale undoes itself.

Radiancy seeps from you in wisdom and beauty.

I don't know how to fully explain the endeavor of

You here, in my life. Forever exceeding the very expectation which has

Followed in its own tampered, flawed, flawless life.

Though in desperate grasp to you, I need not fall,

For you are my balanced compatible being holding me up.

Each papyrus I try to describe my truth to you and my love to you

Yet, the words stumble as I write and an abundance of hope

Provided by yourself in eternal sway and awe.

When lighthouses go up in the fog to provide

Peace, hope, safety, clarity, and eternal guidance,

My belief in you has never faltered and sometimes

We don't even have to communicate. We can
Sit in a room together in silence, and know
Our thoughts and be each other's peace and

Decompressed conversations for life to calm
And be peace and beacon of silence;
A constitution of inspiration you only dream of.

Of course, when I start to feel him wiggle, trying to get
Through the cracks, I must leave and get away.

Raw emotions flourish in eventual standings
And our standards of life with each other grow
To that of the supernatural. I bathe and baske in

Your glory shared by us both and our family;
You are my soul and we shall make holidays
And life blissful and love each bit of it because

I created this blissful paradise of glory for you.
Though I cannot stand and agree with
Suspended thought when you're near.

My everything, my syringa, listen to our heartbeats.
They flutter and flap and slowly whisper every
Breathe we take next to each other.

As I ran back to the witch when he was getting out of control,
I asked her what to do to save you as well and she

Did give one thing. On our wedding night a ritual could help. So when
I get back, we will be married. The road hard, but I knew my

Excitement is in hand, bewildered people stand,
Awe across their face for the raw intensity we
Not only share, but endear every day with

Love we continuously give each other. Every day falling
In love repeatedly with every sunrise and early morning
Breeze. My sunshine, my moon; with you we accomplish

Eternals bliss and truly live in immortality like people
Do with a vampire's kiss. Life's goal is to live and to
Be as great as we possibly can. Yet, you are still dying slowly,

Every day; but I am dying for you to live even more. Dying to live
By your side forever. Even when everything is falling apart,
You're the first thought which calms me down and allows

Me to be able to breathe. When our world gets shaky,
And it gets hard to see a clear ending, you are the breathe
I take to complete my life and our world. Clean and

Perfected in a way only we could put out.
Vows at our wedding were a splendor gave to each other,
but I want to give them to you every day.

You are my only one, I truly love.
I would study the cosmos for you.

I will make you our own universe where we are Gods.
Knowledge is everything in this world,

If I can possess it all, we can rule the universes;
Ours and this one. Your heart's wishes are what will be true.

My forever and always is who you are.
You always take care of me.
Your gentle arms and soft skin allow me to drift to sleep.

Delicate death, inherit my being and allow her to live forever.
In hearts array, be cognisant to a soul dying.
Strength in hand, gliding onto a beauty, decaying

Into the ground after the other half of her soul dies with mine.
Celebration of our lives connected in cosmic reality.
My being slowly brought back from eternal death by your

Sweet nature and love. Blissful warmth, mirror my love.
Shadowed reflections of my full heart, tame our parched
Spirits of the void whilst I am afar.
This world cruel and my presence never
Accepted into the spiritual realm.

You make me triumphant in my victories and allow
Me to pick up my own pieces and that is the greatest
Thing anybody can ask for. Instead of trying to pick them

Up for me, you sat in quiet with me, held me, loved me.
Allowed me to get my things together and be who I am
And this is the only thing people should be able to do.

You know me better than anybody and that should say
How much you mean to me. I do not allow anybody in;
You are the person I not only call my home,

But the person I could ever open up to.
You know everything about me because we have
No secrets. Everything is the truth. I could never lie to you.

My greatest friend, my only true love. Be what it may,
I will have your back and will always do right by you.
I would never want to harm you or hurt you, only to push

You to be the greatest you, the you you've always wanted to be.
The greatest at what you want to do. Eternally and molecularly
My love expands and comes together at the touch and thought

Only you can bring me. My sweet angel, I completely love you.
That word is weird to describe because love is a chemical,
Hence is why we should be able to not only love everyone,

But be able to deplete hate from our lives and our thoughts.
Though, it is true as you know, some people we cannot
Escape from, I cannot escape from. Wasting time and

Energy on people who cannot even fathom what true love
Is. We are true love. You are my true love. My one and only.
You and me, we are to be forever a destiny you cannot split

Or separate, no matter how many times and worlds we fit
Into. This timeline, you are the only thing and person I
Ever hope to accomplish and be with. You are my true

Everything. The one that holds the stars in the sky,
The one that allows mountains to rise.
You are the one. The one who makes everything

Continuously go around and around.
The right and righteous one.
Soul shines brighter than any sun.

Oh, your smile, your laugh.
Your embrace stops my heart
Every time we hug. When I am alone,

Going to sleep, the thought of your embrace
Is what allows me to slowly drift to peace.
Your always in my mind, consuming my life

In a tightly wrapped up love song.
I contagiously and constantly play
You in my mind. Always you, only you.

I only see you. Your beauty and elegance
Stretch across my cosmos and my ongoing
Excellent mind. You are my everything.

Yes, others are pretty, but only certain aspects.
Clothes, hair, eyes, lipstick, only external aspects.
You though, you are absolutely, one hundred percent heavenly.

You're my place where my humbleness and ego lie to sleep.
You are my peace, my silence, my cosmic match.
My heart, made of inspiration of one and loves for

You golden heart. The first thing in my mind
And the last before my eyes shut fully.
I keep falling harder and harder with each passing day.

You are my light when dark fog seems
To be the only thing I can see. Trueness
And destiny lights up anyone interfering.

Your perfume sustains my emotions
To one in harmonized sequencations.
Equivalent and even my energy

Is back to being right. The best part
Of my day is seeing you and it stretches
Upon my face in such an obvious way.

Red lights my cheeks and my eyes sparkle
Inside your brightly lit eyes. Your eyes make
My heart stutter and flutter like a nervous bee.

Absolute hunger and desire lurks from me to you
And motivation; intelligence furthers my ability
To be able to self sustain in your beauty and

Intuition. I desperately try to catch up in your world
Keeping ahold of everything you and I deserve along
The way. The universe and cosmos is what it might be.

I work to afford to get to that point. A point where
I am good enough and can reach that level of
Love and life. For I shall always support and honor

You. You. You deserve whatever joyful and
Beautiful love this eternal world can offer.
Growth and prosperity allows us to gain

Everything we have and will always want out of life.
Thinking about what this could succumb to;
My heart races and my blood raises

Awaiting your Angelic voice providing
Essence and love. My life and my love,
You are my everything, my Angel and

The very being who challenges every
Aspect of my being. If life was this glorious;
Rates of death would drop instantly.

Death beseeched all those who have
Came before you. None have touched
Your raw inspirational beauty at hand.

Inspiration seeps from you as disbelief
Causes cancer to those who try to be you.
There is only one you so you cannot be

Copied or turned into something she is not.
You are the pinnacle operation of desire
And the one who makes everyone else

Wish they were you. Every tiny aspect of your
Eyelashes and nails makes others squirm in
Their own skin. How deliberate

Your elegance is. Such pretty mastery.
The calm radiancy stinges your accuracy
Of knowledge and perfected elegance.

Your ravishing etiquette makes for
A blissful mix with intelligence. Nothing
Can separate the bonding of two

Intricate chemicals. Bonding of each
Of us makes for a stunning eclipsing
Balance when our two cosmos meet.

Gentle and soft our glorious beings
Have ached for something quiet.
Our shining stars have been

Raging for peace for as long as we have
Combined our souls for an epic; only desired
For a longing and rejoicing love. Acquitted of

Hardships unknown to a world unfit
For a passion so unbearable and a love
Completely contested in a time where

Only selfish wars happen inside of
This tainted species. For a long time
Love was something only lust could

Comprehend. Wanting to hurry along to
Be grown and be something in a darkened
World; yet my brilliance now, only sees what

Light and beauty now offers. Our hunger
Arches for a rolling beauty only you
Can offer them. My muse. My love.

Everything we have achieved and everything
We work to attain and have; is the invincibility
Of hearts and lives of people trying to reach,

And yet, people strive to achieve the originality
We have; the gods we are.
We rule the galaxies and the cosmos.

People look to us to rule and we rule eternity.
When you are here we dedicate our love to
The family we hope to create; spreading

Passion over the endless eternities.
Even through my darkest times
Your light continues to shine bright.

It glares through my darkness and as you hold me
I know after this time is over, I shall have to carry
Myself forward and build myself up on my own.

You allow your light to shine around me and
Protect my pieces from falling through the universe.
As I pick them up you are there allowing space,

Room for growth and inspiration for my newly
Better self. Shedding my old skin; growing a new
Layer, allowing me to better prepared for dealing

With such darkening matters of death and decaying.
I smile at your blushed cheeks as my head reaches
From your chest to kiss your cheek during our star gazing

Night. You're the reason for a continued persistence
At being the greatest this world has seen. You are the
Reason my love has been unshaken and the depths

Of my perspiring rain of forever love; just like the eternity
Of cosmos and forever tranquility and peace. My radiant
Angel, you are forever the perfect love of the most sincere

Raw, pure form. Truly a radiancy pleasure. You are
A reason for continuity. You make everything
Easier to deal with. I know death is hard, but with love

It is very much bearable. You are the inspiration
Of my inspiration. Continuance of our circumferenced
Mind stimulates the moral references of our honesty.

You my darling, are the light in my eyes,
The decay in my softened attitude. Dazzling as ever,
You continue to stun. Though genius is still growing

And the willingness to learn is something that's never done.
Engraving a highly cumulative intelligence of manners
And suspenseful magnificence. You are the radiance

Of everything perfect in this deliciously painted world.
The sky neigh, sun setted upon the delayed
Consequence of the tainted beings of their darkened estate.

You and I; we are completely free of every chain
Contaminated upon our ankles and wrists. No stress,
No sadness, no depressed algorithms. You and I,

Just living a continuous elegant life.
The ongoing normalcy in this world
Is the only disease spreading in this

Wretched yet kind world.
The dismal beings taint
Your brilliancy. You bait

People into the elegance of a soft touch.
The groan of these people feeling bad
Are everything of your ravishing familiaralities.

Intrigued beauty of desirable worth,
You are the only measurable work
Of art that is sustainable on a journey

Of equitable measure. Measure upon matters
Is something we can contribute; though after
These dazzled constraints are we going to be through?

Is all this going to end when the glint
In the stars stale out our stylish form?
When we are done and dead are you

Going to be by my side at the end?
Once we are done with the intelligence,
With the beauty, with everything,

Are we going to continue this glorious love
We are currently making? This troubling
Thought aches and echoes in the bright

Lights of our room. Is the coincidences
Of our weird nature expire after the
Bright cosmos's come to an end?

Gratitude storms the dangerous echoes
From a charisma of reflected shadows.
When the mirrors break in our darkened

Room and you see the broken me and
I see the broken you, will we still love
The beings we fell in love with, or will

Our desiccated God beings be able to
Stick out the love we have found in our
Past selves. Aging is a distracting way of

Being able to keep the posh civilness
We practice to master; but if we are
Not still growing, will we still make each

Stronger? When the moon strikes
The night and the sun seizes the day,
Will we still walk this eternal love?

Soft and touching the transparency
Of the wind full of love and happiness,
Shall fall in the anguish of time and

Killer decorations of this tainted bloody grave.
You and I will stay entangled forever, for how
Could you and I ever separate our raw and

Purified bond? When we start clicking on every
Molecule, I shall ask you and we should always
Be challenging ourselves. Our broken

Mirror shall show us the light in our cornered
Rooms. How these long and blissful nights
Seem like nothing to a singing masterpiece

Backed by a symphony or an orchestra
We shall forever rage in this normal world
We so desperately try to call home. Everyone but you

And I; we make this world ours,
Continuing to elevate this particular
Loving portraits we make of each other.

Inscrutable from others, desperate in others,
We continuously guide the installations
With our over spilling glamor and dedication

To flatter and be this world's roses
And tulips. Love is anxious and love is
Gentle, soft. Love is everything beautiful.

You are everything beautiful in this world.
You are gentle, soft. You are everything.
You are the particles, the galaxies, in this

Already impeccable world. You are life and
Death in this world. Angelic in sight and
Loss of ego for a perfect balance of selfish

And selflessness. You are balance of
Everything good and bad. You are
Light and dark. One hundred percent

Equal, yet all light is shined through
Any dark pieces of this insanity of a world.
Delightful and peaceful, your raw purity

Is shown through all that is around you.
Brilliance in glory. Such stamina in a
Deck of foreshadowed people around you.

Magnificence spills from you like an over-
Flowing water fountain that cannot keep
Contain life's full coins. Elegance seeps

From the genius you prosper by.
Extravagance tips the balance
Of all those who will be estranged

In a trained and flawless beauty
This world has put into you.
Enduring thoughts portray what you

Always thought this world should
Be. Perfection whispers through
The wind and comes upon us.

This walk giving foresight

Of the mornings breeze shaping

This next world of success and love.

Part Two: Writings throughout History

I closed off Osiris and he died,
Egypt then turned to desert and the world
Fell silent. Now I must save my poisoned love.

I can create this mirror verse though.
I can save her. I can save my mind.

These years have passed, you are still there.
The battle with Osiris has fallen away,
For these pages have disappeared

To what it seems like in history.
My blockade in my mind tamed
To where it eroded and broke. It tears

Into my being, condemning me to losing
Pieces of me. Everyday becomes harder,
But if I can figure out how to make a world

To save you I will. The wedding ritual
Only slowed down your poisoned soul,
So this world can save us both.

You are the one to unlock my fullest
Potential. Your hospitality of my soul
Enraged my being to continuously

Become the greatest, most intelligent
Of all species, even those aliens in the
Sky circling the confidence of everything

Which is all immaculate greatness.
You are the inspired being of everything
Which has come to all those before.

My mind clear for months and yet
Regret strains it now. I put you in danger
And I cannot fix you. I cannot get

You were not meant to live forever;
Neither was I, but it worked for me,
Why didn't it work for you?

This world building right. They bust and burn
And time is nowhere on our side. Your body
Decaying, becoming more and more frail.

Time slips by and bonding escaping
Our gentle conspiracies. Expressing
A love, only eternal, dignities

Of prosperity only fair for those of immortality.
Achieved and proclaimed the self sincerity
Laminated in a time of misconceived territory

Of a connected universe conceived of a time, decorated
With brilliance and inspiration of a time holding constraints,
Of a cold, Alaskan night.

Our diapason is uninterrupted
In concrete sincerity, my love gives stationed in a constitute
Of reasoning, beyond belief and hysteria of your love.

Reasoning of responses and recollection in continuity and demise
Of others love. My complete true singular being. My enduring specimen.
Limitations stretch the opposing hearts as your pure, white alluring being

Taints the after effect of enduring life and love to me. These others cannot
Keep up with the constant war we wage on life's luring, diminishing grasp
On everyday souls.

You and I will unlock
the full human potential.
Swerving in and out of extravagant

Offers and finding and finishing the ones we
Bless to be our favorites. Life is already something
We as a race make way harder than necessary.

What if this was all a game? A simulation?
Would you want every day to be hard or stressed in this
Already shortened life? Would you want it to be

Filled with desire and emotions?
The warmth your arms and heart provide,
Are the same these desires and emotions

Guide me to. These tendencies and consistencies
Overreach my bearings of hope and beauty
In a charismatic manor of grace.

Studying the slight hymns from praises
Only sung to you. The mountain's foot

Embarking on only those which comes from real root.

When we went to study Achilles to try to make you a God

yourself, he saw our passion and love which
Guided his own hands to be love which ended
Up killing him. Seems like love has done nothing

But kill and yet, you and I won't be killed by it.
We are strength and determination
And when glass turns to sand so will our bodies.

Dying biblically is the only thing which can
Suffice for our olden being which lusts for
A glorious life filled with your love like my love for you.

Your soul, old at heart, young in being,
Lightens my every being; being able to hold
Your soft hand. On my lap I hold you, cherish you.

Your eyes are still trying to flutter open and it is my eyes you first see again.
Head clearer now than before and suddenly your aching
Is completely gone. I have healed your heart, soul, mind and body.

Frustrating prophecies come to me and only one
I want to come true. As they start to come true
Every time I close my eyes and see you; I hope when

They open you are the one who continuously shows the truth.
You are the only one I wish to endure over and over again.
Your warmth is the only thing I want to ever feel again.

Your warmth is something that covers me in clarity
And gives me a blanket which surrounds me with joy
And eternal bliss. What wonderful peace.

Yet, these prophecies will not halt and deteriorate
For my mind has continued growing them like seeds,
And you are the only one which is simplistic love.

Achilles Note on Love

They carry my tortured hands and feet throughout

History while granting us terrible names. When I wake

Soul after soul is given my sacrifice all over the world.

Everyone who believed in us in the old world has now

Suffered the ill fate I have. These feelings naked and exposed.

You shall be strung in the chambers of desolate darkness

Condemned by your masters sins and sending millions of

People to flee the great state you hail from. When the master

Is murdered you shall be the sole reason of millions of deaths.

Although, not all bad, you saved the lives of more.

This path was not at all for faint of heart, for science will

Be ahead by hundreds of years thanks to you;

Though if you come I fear you will not be coming

Back, not permanently. Your nature justified in

Erratic states of mind slowly to deteriorate

In a state of confusion. All will be lost, but only

Because great sacrifices were made.

Only you will know when the end is nye,

Yet you will not know the precise time you

Will come to this darkened time frame.

No one here will remember you, but you will

Live on infamously. Straddle and tossed you shall

Fear, but that rocking boat will never halt.

Is it too late to protest this? Is your path already

Set upon? You turn back now, everything will be lost.

My eyes jolted open, for I stretched upon the bed to find you.
Your warmth radiates to me, giving warmth
And sign that you are okay.

Our love grows deeper and we continue to
Achieve and unlock our deeper potentials and meanings.
We see we can continuously expand intellectually,

Continuously exceed anybody's expectations.
Our story underlined in these outlandish
Propositions, shadowing my ongoing heart to you.

Nothing could hold back what I will give to you.
Passion condemned while your eyes
In sight, my hand in yours.

Smooth tables stack as our comfortability levels
Grow more and more with slight smiles
And glances we give each other.

It seems like every time a glance is given
It cannot be taken back. Mind rolls over
Many personalities and yet it keeps

Running over and over; most of it saying
Nearly the same thing. Trying to show passion,
My soul urging vulnerability stretching

To a profound effect, I myself, cannot comprehend
Sometimes. My mind glamorous, yet your stunningness
Makes my mind too cloudy to think.

These scars cover my body are the same stitches
My mind covers up as the dark history
Clumps from my mouth trying to get out.

I continuously try and write you in these tales and poems
And nothing can sustain a beauty like yours.
Words cannot try and move from my mouth.

My mind is nowhere from these suspended skies.
Delicate as they are, they still fail to hold my love.
Even when I make a world for you it fails

As does my mouth. It cannot further open
As it continuously stays shut in the eternal
Forever my pen writes.

Occasionally I succeed, but the beauty I need
To describe you, is a pain no words can explain.
My mind aches; how you were kind enough to marry me;

Yet I cannot locate what word I could use
To come close to tell you how deeply I am in love with you.
Stunning, astonishing, electrifying are words; the closest

I can use to describe my love filled heart, yet you exceed all
These capabilities and expectations laid before you.
Though, passionate about family first,

I am stuck in the middle of a cycle, I wear
Nervousness upon my face. My heart pounds

And it is strange you cause this, yet it is only you,

Who is able to substantiate these feelings and pounding.
Our wonder for not only each other, but this world can never
Cease. Nothing can stand in the way of our love. Whether we

Do this through intellectual, philosophical debates,
Or whether we do this with our child like spirits.
One thing though is for sure, and this is, I

Will never lie to you. You, my one and only.
Never could I lie fully to people, but you I will never
Lie to. Everyone's incompetence gives me a

Reason to not tell the full truth, but to smartly talk
In a way down to the ignorance people correspond with.
The intuition and competence you have bestowed upon

Yourself, is true rarity. Processing your endeavoring
Preferences I make way to your locked down heart;
In caged, on lockdown for good reason, you gently

Allow me more and more information. My heavy attraction
To you is not just physically, but spiritually and emotionally,
Every day is a new challenge opening up to you.

That night runs through my head, have I caused you to get worse?
Have I killed us both? The words ring through my being:

Delicate death, inherit my being and allow her to live forever.
In hearts array, be cognisant to a soul dying.

Strength in hand, gliding onto a beauty, decaying

Into the ground after the other half of her soul dies with mine.
Celebration of our lives connected in cosmic reality.
My being slowly brought back from eternal death by your

Sweet nature and love. Blissful warmth, mirror my love.
Shadowed reflections of my full heart, tame our parched
Spirits of the void whilst I am afar.
This world cruel and my presence never
Accepted into the spiritual realm.

You, my love, will never change my tempted heart.
How flesh strips its century old lust for
beings and yet here you are, still, my dear old love.

I could never leave you, you could never leave me.
My heart and soul are bounded to yours eternally;
As the cosmic beings and reality have ceased

My understanding of life itself, yet, at its center,
You are their, my head on your chest and
Our hands intertwined together.

Systems derange and my mind stabilizes from the insane.
Abstract thoughts now damaged and concrete images
Cracking my god-like brain.

You have changed the world for me, so I shall for you.
An abstract continuity to a more fortified being.
Every time our hands touch the sensations

Give me a chill of such a wonderful dedication.
Pleasant tranquilities ring through my head
As I pin down why I continue to fall more and more in love

With every beat of our collected heart.
Out of everyone in their sheltered lives,
You and I seemed to be the only ones

Who are no longer terrified to live a full life,
While sharing in emotions and conversations
With a like mind and purpose.

How I could love you this completely; I
Do not know. I do not understand how these
Feelings can arise in such a delicate way.

My love cannot be explained nor can your
Beauty, yet I am here trying to describe an
Interstellar human being.

If I could figure out how I could live without you,
Maybe I wouldn't drag myself all over the world
Trying to save you and countless worlds

Being created and destroyed, when we find
Out, it cannot hold you. Many wasted and patience worn,
One of these must work or gone you will be.

As I continuously write your world
All which comes to mind is the beauty

Of reflections and mirrors of our eternal love.

After Osiris and Achillis and Zeus,
They must be correct to you may always be
Out of reach, for you are getting worse,

Yet still some patience yearns in me.
These days may be numbered and may not
Work forever, but you and I shall live a happy life together.

I wish the intensified studying with these philosophers
Of ancient Greece and those who came afterwards taught me how to stop the cracking.
One more world. One more then I shall take a break.

Impossible to write about and yet when I create,
The only thing which seeps from mind, are
Your beauty and your excellence which creeps

From the knowledge which is based deep within you.
My intellect springs out more intellect and our world
Is created based on your love for me.

Bright and flourishing it seeps through.
You gaze around to everybody worshiping you.
In this new world you are our goddess, but when it comes to

You and me; you are my goddess every day.
Love for each other mimicked for our gimmicks,
And a world unified by your ultraviolet ways.

Our love more real than ever, even in a world
Made for you. This world will hold
My love and everything I stand for, for you are

My syringa, my passion. My muse has only
Been settled upon to you. For without you my
Smile and dedication lost in histories palace

Of exile. A purgatory only those made from the Hells can visit.
You are the purity of laughter and the love of this world
Is going to be forever yours to love and honor.

The only thing that could come close is when
You look up at the stars and see the northern lights;
When you look up galaxies and cosmos are pictured,

The beauty and eternality each of these pictures
Possess, are with such magnificence in color is how your
Beauty, intelligence and my love can be compared.

This perfect creation is finished and everything
Looks normal, yet in order to save you, I have
To sacrifice my own mind. I cannot save my head,

But I can save you. This universe is mirrors and
Reflections, built upon your love for me, since everything
Else failed, including my love to you.

My soul becomes more and more black
As it becomes evident that Osiris's death
Has left me terribly ill. I plan for my end.

Chapter Three:
New World Writings

Our lives have lived strong
Throughout this new world.
Doubt was stricken from my mind

Until this papyrus were laying signed
In my arms saying the tale was lost
To history, yet, here I am, in it.

This story is real. Poetic justice lived
Long in my blood. Where is my being?
In the graveyard with my ex,

Back in Egypt all those years ago?

Here it is, your deathbed and yet
You fight for every second your body
Can possibly give you.

Chest tightening, throat burning, hard breathing.
Eyes flutter open and closed and it is I
Who continues to sustain an environment

Of youth and prosperity. Long gone and death
Upon your skin. Nothing interferes with your death
And yet, it is I who can't handle the chance of death.

Our immortality is
Supposed to free us from being these
Different characters, these ants, humans.

When I made my love's cosmos, it certainly

Was enveloped with the charisma you engulf
To allow love and certainty to spread across the world.

My heart lifts and falls like a ride and my nerves sink in my throat
As I choke trying to tell you these words about
Constellations; how they arise every time you are near.

Our love which has been guided throughout
History has brought you to this new world with
Me, and it is here where you can relax.

Your eyes are flawless as they
Flutter open. Shining as bright as the sun,
We have fully made it. We are together

In every category. Your dreams hail you to a place
You've never been before. I just want to be yours forever.
Would you be mine if I decorated your heart with my soul?

My love though, never yields, but grows
Blossoming into a dominate life where all those
Who surround are their to help support and bolster

Your life into cherished simplistic love.
I know this is not our own world,
For after many attempts, this one stops

Your terrible disease from continuous spreading;
But it is here where we can live our full life.
The origin world has become too violent in this

New century. Only here can we still be our
Ordinary selves hailing from great Egypt.
I know you can't repair their world,

But this world will never try to bleed apart.
We can live here for as long as my heart
Beats for they will worship you. I shall make sure of this.

Colors fluorescent in sight, yet it helps to
Slow the blaring disease he has caused you.
We dreamed of humans no longer near,

Yet everything begins to become clear.
You jump and twirl for everything has
Become back to normalcy. You start

To feel your bones take fold back to where
They should have been back in the known
World. This world decorated with gardens

And have been inspired by love.
Our love for each other. I deepen
In passion and our love never ceases.

Stress and frustration dissipated from sight.
Our lives arched in glorious becomings, basking
In the new found glory of this home.

When the world couldn't hold us
And it ended, this began to hold you.
It is continuity at its finest.

The cosmos are funny that way.
When I picked you and belief faltered in Osiris;
The day came and as it dragged to night,

The waves carried away and the sand from the bottom
Of the ocean had then turned Egypt into a state of chaos
And dust. When we went to study Achilles trying to make you a God

Yourself, he saw our passion and love which
Guided his own hands to be love which ended
Up killing him. Seems like love has done nothing,

But kill, and yet, you and I won't be killed by it.
We are strength and determination,
And when glass turns to sand so will our bodies.

A biblical death is the only thing which can
Suffice for our olden beings, which lusts for
A glorious life filled with your love like my love for you.

Your soul, old at heart, yet young in being.
It lightens my every being; being able to hold
Your soft hand in mine. On my lap I hold you, cherish you.

Your eyes are still trying to flutter open and it is my eyes you first see again.
Head clearer now than before and suddenly your aching
Is completely gone. I have healed your heart, soul, mind and body.

Frustrating prophecies come to me and only one
I want to come true. As they start to come true

Every time I close my eyes and see you I hope when

They open you are the one who continuously shows the truth.
You are the only one I wish to endure over and over again.
Your warmth is the only thing I want to ever feel again.

Your warmth is something that covers me in clarity
And gives me a blanket which surrounds me with joy
And eternal bliss. What wonderful peace.

Yet, these prophecies will not halt and deteriorate
For my mind has continued growing them like seeds,
And you are the only one which is simplistic love.

How can I wander through this world alone, when you
Inspire every inch of my soul and every star and galaxy alike.
Every God has found love and I have now found mine.

Every tightly knitted line and rhyme inner, molecular, and all others
Are like my never ending love for you. Until these stars fall
And rain moves upward, until the clouds cease to entertain

The blue, cool, sky. Forever love like the sun blasts
Its energy out into the world. Until oceans drain and
Trees no longer mold the ground, my love will

Sustain and never deteriorate.
Sarcoma was in her chest,
We barely caught it before she entered death.

Forward attempts at flattery fall on blushed cheeks.

Engaging desires leaving us always wanting more.
Hunger sustains mutual beings for love

I've never accounted for. Love wild and intact.
Our connection grows deeper and more sincere
On each level. Starting as a child, love, has

Turned more than flatters. A mutual respect
Of work and dedication. Mind boggles at every
Connection. Mind always containing more

Intelligence as we try for complete
Originality; in our relationship and what we strive for.
Attempts at making our work become easier as we

Fall more in love and intact with our feelings
Overarching of principles taint what other have done; we though,
Are trying for raw, rapid love and desire we

Maintain. As distractions fall upon us, they are waived
Away as we are our own desires. Love isn't structured;
It's wild, rapid, chaotic, chemicals that bond and explode.

It's the exact opposite of a polished work of art.
Love is displayed like a masterpiece which it can be; but it is
Also something gentle and messy. No one likes to capture that.

You; you challenge me to capture everything. Making
Me a better writer and honest being. We are filled
Of glorious spectacles; yet we as humans choose

To not unlock our untapped potential.

Our minds, you and I, are always clicking at full capacity.

We just have to reach more every day and some

Of our growth will be of natural habits, like you.

Natural growth with those around you. Not as a follower

Though, always as a leader. Challenging everyone to

Continuously grow on your behalf.

Even as death grows near and people die,

You allow me to pick me up and grow alongside

You without punishing me or trying to pick me up yourself.

True love is what I have when I am with you.

Desperate to maintain the troubled balance

Which has restored its natural context.

We continue to live through the being,

rising through the depths, for we shall

Forever inherit the grasping concept of concrete

Love and aspects of every day life.

We continue to march on leading the way.

These tiny specimens seem to continually

Go down a path of continuity and distaste.

You though, you inspire and devote consistencies

To travel the world with prosperity, love and care.

Empathetic caresses every place you visit

And people have become sympathetic

To the embraced love you and I share.
It spreads wide and is unending just like
The cosmos we share in our forever

Untapped potential minds. We spread
Our growth and our prosperity
To all those places we visit.

You are an essential part of
This transparent world. You and I
Have no secrets and we shall

Never lie to each other.
Our endeavoring modesty
Sparks our beautiful reflections

In the shards of glass staining
The broken mirror upon our floor.
You are the strike of a grenade

That breaks this earth. You are the
Peace that brings this earth into
One symmetrical place to thrive.

This cherished world will surround many
Of those who have yet to take their first
Steps and those who

Will be taking their lasts. Contaminated
In death's love and heart filled with warmth,

Our guidance stretches far and spreads

Worlds away. Galaxies sting and loosen
When relaxed upon our trusted words.
Your world gripping together by our thoughts and phrases.
Taints of rust speck across this entangled

Difference in stained time; but love rains
Through the bling of despair and stretches
The continuity of loss and deprived hope.

Stinge of sadness aches the desecrated
Beings of death in a coffin, yet, as the
Doors blow open and the bitter cold

Taints the chilled echo of what your beauty
And love has bit away. The sting of death
No longer pains the wounds of despair.

Even as each second ticks and your heart
No longer beats, my love keeps you breathing.
Tainted in a hug, the embrace seemingly

Washes away everything this pain paints for you.
Painting despair, anguish, torture, I can barely
Deal with the emotions of loss and yet what I can

Deal with, is an unbearable amount of paralysis
Which now stops your body from hurting. Stretching
Upon the forced ending and beginning; we shall learn

Our mistakes were only meant for gracious love.
Jokes beseech in our final moments together,
You dig deep into my arms and hang on like nails

To a cliff, not wanting to let go, yet, you know you must.
Saving your life my breath allows us to live eternally.
Your brilliancy in your eyes I now see knows I did right.

The one who doesn't play victim. The one who has complete
Control of her life. The one who takes the power and owns it.
These people play the part, but my love, you work for everything.

Seamlessly perfected upon a conscious only desired
To be challenged and applauded for being pushed
And for the guarded soul. Our essence echos to the after worlds

And only they realize the truth only painted by true love's repair.
Aspirations dawn intensified passion in a world lacking
Both attributes. Last to continuously grow. Our triumphs are

Stupendous. Nothing can contribute or contract
Our tremendous, molecular connection. Just like
These structured paragraphs, our character sharp;

Tightly knitted. Our metaphysical beings breeches the beseech
Culture trying to cage us in. Our souls are strengthened
Between us and our inspirations of delicate decay.

This world has taught us we should make and rule our own life.
By your Angelic strength are we able to achieve. Only deserving pearls
and greatness,

You lie in immortality. Giving growth between you and the molecules

Which guides your being for health and intelligence.
Mentality always engaging and momentum forever
Swinging and swaying on and on into galaxies and the cosmos.

Even those who are built to reign and bathe
Of the glory profounded by your continued
excellence. Every person not touched by your

Presence is blanketed in stress and dismay of the loudness
Life brings. Boasts and ignorance are posted of normally
This world desecrates. Beauty and peace no longer

Sustained in the heart of this world.
Sensations spark interests in these mirror worlds;
Breaking the glass in universes departing lost souls

To their ancient love. You inherently take the responsibility
To help love connections take their true forms once again.
These people back to their loves, but your humbleness indeeds

Portrays the last chivalry people used to have.
Your love and the cherish you bring is the true
Indication of your brilliant connections. Your eyes

Light up and sparkle every time you laugh.
When you are here and love is in the air,
I worship your beauty just like everyone

Else in this world does.

I cannot wait
To hold you every night, love you every day,

Be your life with every waking moment.
Heart aching, your touch healing, how
You are my everything.

Hearts sustaining joy as you continue to be
My soul, my absolute, complex, entirety.
You are my complete dictionary.

In awe, my awe is your awe.
Marriage has been everything we could
Have dreamt of and more. For when I think

About you my heart races and a smile
Sharp upon my face. You make my thoughts
Dissipate by your smile and quiet giggle.

All this time, you are the only thing which comes to mind.
I wish upon all words I could describe you,
But this is something I cannot do, simply because

Words are not enough to describe you.
This olden language we have yearned for
Is as comprehensible and beautiful as you can be.

The lofty language we used to use when we
Wrote poetry together, is the one I should be using when
Talking about you. You are my only true desire.

Our poetry is, as etiquette, and simply done
As your gracious beauty and precious love.
Our ancient souls belong back in

Time when inspiration had its own simple
And majestic calling. Beauty has lifted our
Blissful image and maintains a collective purity.

Affirmations stick to strike the ones
We love and care down and yet,
You and I are cool and delicate.

We cannot dictate cruelness set upon by others,
And yet, we love everything about this world.
The stress we used to feel is now nothing.

Decorated alongside these people
We help them maintain a level of security
As they thrive. These poetic justices

Take place over centuries of work. You and I
Have shared such terrible passings, relating
Us back to the olden days. Now we rule the world,

Stretching our love to the end of our
Combined cosmos's, yet, the light shines past
Through all eternity, finding no end in all the worlds,

Galaxies. Achieving worlds of honor I bring you
Only what you deserve, greatness, dignity and honor.
Everything this life has and needs to offer.

We have lifted these sections and with this world, now old,
Our love has embarked this place for hundreds of years
As I glide all over every world, trying to find you the cure.

I have searched the sides of every talented scientist.
Each one demanding a little bit of your blood to
Try and figure out this ancient disease which haunts

My thoughts. For I can bounce back and forth between
These worlds, yet, you cannot. If you cross back
Instant death awaits you. This curse though, someone has to know

A cure from the deceased God.
Days go by sometimes where I drag my feet,
Attempting to get this right, for you, for us.

Arching crosses urge each monotonous movement
To every diamond on this planet whispering your
Name, while liquor smooth, slides down the throat

Of an alcoholic, looking up at us from far.
My heart and my soul; you are the vision
Or my dreams. You are my visionary.

As such, sometimes my mind is trapped in the broken
Fragmentations of our past life. The alcohol I brought
Into our world to remind us of some kind of normalcy

As our homeland is torn apart, yet, this only makes me suffer
More, for I wish the liquor was sliding down

My throat, just like back in the day.

Elegance sustains you as you allow movements
From people within a telling torment.
People go and come and you help them find

The peaceful light you have created since
This universe was brought to you. Beginning of time
And here we are, still standing tall as can be.

A barrier like the great corrals. Beautiful and awe
Striking. You are much like these. We stand together,
Yet you shall always grace me by being equal

In existence. You though, are still and will always
Stand on a pedestal throughout our forever, ongoing,
Awe inspiring, existence. Shined in the glowing

Tone of excelled growth in intelligence.
We bathe and baske in elegance and
Correct the world of its terrible deeds.

Some allow murder to foreshadow and without
This, we could not have her healed in this mirror
Verse. Broken fragments are the things that heals

Her. As these deeds are corrected though, her condition
Seems to slowly creep up in her cemented bones.
Our lives are well into the thousands, and still, we are fragile.

The groove of our rule allows you to be

Everywhere and the pedestal does shine.
Your blush comes through your gentle

Cheeks. How we all love and portray
Little aspects of your complete array.
Tiny pieces of who you are is remnant

In everyone who sees you and tries
To be better and maintain a flawless,
Raw image. Restless in the night we strive

To be what you will always be,
The being everyone wants to be.
You are the expectation.

You and I shall share this universe together,
And together we shall rule infamously
Upon a world so gathered by light and beauty already.

You are the portrait of this world.
The instincts of this world.
The overall beauty and blessings of this world.

Etiquette of your elegance stretching in a detailed
Rumbling of hearts to match. Your name fills in my lungs
With love and hope in times of continued hardship.

Rebranding names, people, things, times and growth
With a partner which takes even longer. The old Roman
Saying: "Fortune favors the brave." You make me brave.

This is who we are. We are the brave. We are the power.
We are the excellence, the elegant. You are my everything.
You are my Angel. My one and only. My life's cosmos.

Condemned for my actions in life, people come to see me
trying to mend their unscarred relationships with me.
Yet it is you who see these people don't get

The satisfaction of friendship when I lay here dead.
How the love of my life became eternal and in death I wait
For you on the plane in death. Whether accepted in any Heaven

Or any Hell we should be in. How confidence urges
Us to be tested in all waters, you my love,
Will always be by my side.

Deceiving and decaying my eyes lay blame in
My deepening heart. The party we shall see

Will be one where we storm the gallows and pits
To true paragons of hope, love and tranquility.
Peace sets upon my mind as I think about you again.

To hear your voice and yet it is not your voice I get.
Life flies by and we do not know it is over until us
Immortal beings get scared and nervous of whatever

Afterlife we are guided to. Beliefs carry much weight,
Though, they are not waived by the gentleman standing
By such weight. My guided philosophies have me on

Borders of my failed universes all strung together
Like a bridge I can cross if I ever fully commit.
My love, you and I shall rule eternity every day and the

Glorious sightings shall all be interwoven in our
One true prosperity afterlife. You and I shall forever
Continue in a delicate manuel, foreshadowed

By the pit in our stomachs telling us to continue
Making this glorious place of birth and death.
Only the ones we contest of the most beautiful

And gentle souls can pick a guided existence after
This delicate process. You gave me the purpose and
Prosperity I needed to continue to motivate in this

Continued universe. Breaking and continuing I shriek
In the face of troubled existence until your hand interlocks
With mine we see full, true power. Though thanks to foresight

I've seen the death beseeching our understanding before
It's unnervingly happening. Instead of telling you though,
I hold it inside trying to allow my heart to do what it says.

You have created for me this place for death, like Valhalla
And our Gods and the new Gods combined.
These appeasing and inspiring my new being.

Noticing I haven't been me lately, you gift me this afterlife.
The best present anyone could give me, is this that you have given to me.
Our last exchange, nothing meaningful and yet as I tell you

Inside another safe in my fully guarded and protected mind.
You are the key and the sanctuary of the fully stretched
Alien ideology of my most sincere mentality.

My love will grace her presence and all those bathing in the
Sunlight of her presence, shall be healed automatically by
Her rays of eternal glow and forever sighting a cleansing mind.

Your eyes and body are my continued destiny.
You are my continued presence to live in harmony
And the echoing of glass and reflections upon the glass

Look back at me in a pretentious way. They know and are
Jealous of our reign for eternity; guiding the cosmos's to
Forever glory and prosperity. I stand taller than ever next to

You and your being of magical splendor.
Our prestigious haunts a sentimental life
Which is overshadowed by the continued

Excellence of a dominating specter of
Eager connections on our molecules
Which is now starting to guide us into a

Single mind, which will be, a harmonized effect
Of complete undying love we have for each other.
Stirring in a module and this inscrutable head

Of mine, the only thing completely clear is the love
We share for each other and the awe-inspiring shock

I feel as our hands and arms glide together in the embrace

Of a complex and gentle warmth between us and our
Replica of gain and bowing excellence of eternal devotion.
Our complex structures embark on a spectacle so

Overdone by architects, we face the songs in our hearts
Telling us our souls are the same. When we combine in
Glamor the worlds of our cosmos combine into one;

And the paradise you created is perfected with
This last combination of our hungered love
We continuously feed each other.

The split seconds the cosmos stopped breathing
We were able to restart everyone's heart automatically.
Successful in its entailed energy our details

Were simultaneously exact to that of every
World before creation of humanity.
Fully stimulated we continuously surge our
Forgotten anthems these cosmos were guided by.

You and I in full display of what love should be in its
Eternal beating heart. We are the fundamental sound
Of what love should not only be, but the way love

Is and will always be handled. It is gracious, yet,
It is a complex language we have learned to
Master and forever use to explain the difficulties

Which are hard for the everyday person to understand.
We are the sound of echos and the utility of radioactive
Chemicals lighting up the worlds in this universe.

We know what is happening and yet it plays out
Because if love was to interfere with free will,
It would not be love after all.

Although these things are real, nothing can
Impact the way your love continues to attach
And grow upon my flesh and into my heart.

The calling we have upon our hearts
Consistently rage throughout the galaxies;
Continuing to grow stronger and

Impress even ourselves as our love will
Outshine any darkness we have stringed
Upon us in our multitude of laughter.

Syringa, we have entangled in our softly
Corrupting temptations of forever escapement
Of our minds into the mold we have and

Eternally will always adapt. The inspiration
We coherently race until normalcy is erased
From our memory. Only the ongoing race for

Unconventional remarkability, is the essence
Of the impeccable nature we continuously
Aim to achieve in this galaxy of tangled beauty.

We flourish in our brilliance of untainted, yet,
Sensationable attributes to allow our insatiable
Ideas to continue to flow steadily throughout the universe.

Our being cannot be broken or molded to fit
Anyone of our highly accrued intelligence.
Suppressed in an entangled box of psychotic

Melodies raise in the wrangled beings of our love.
Raced in an unearthly presence of an occasional
Lack of normalcy. We arc of excellence and refute

The normalcy; the lack of understanding of
The entire mediocrity of which these ordinary souls
Have abided by since the start of every cosmic world.

Beings of estranged thoughts
Radiate my mind into a tangled
Perfection of my labyrinth mind.

Winter setting promptly

In the town and the warmth of your embrace stitch
The towns clouded judgment and memories
Only warmth by you and the soft finches

Song. Fluttering through clouds and trees, this pass deluded
With past memories and solemn nights. People now use
Pictures to portray their emotions towards the world as

Anguish develops in your strengthened heart. As it withers
And windes away, we can only beat it for so many days.
Our departure sets the town to below freezing heights

And with no precautions from your warmth going out
People start to die and their paths wonder from a golden
Road leading up to our house where warmth in continuity

Shifts to a frozen wasteland, unbearable by those
Who shed no tears. I cannot go out and protect them
Since the salty water hasn't left my cheek in far too

Long. Your bleeding heart has you in tears across
The floor in true torment and despair. You turn and toss
Until the light we have shared for so long,

Turned itself into the solemn, darkened depths of our hearts.
I too fear these feelings will ache me down and my determination
Has shown the piety where to be grown to a flowery happiness

Yet even they die in the chair of dismay and heartache.
This sadness; too unbearable I can no longer crush them
With my wit and soul, but they start to leak up to my throat;

And this anxiety we share all too well cannot be back;
For this was abolished years ago in the depths of the blackened moat
Which is protected by the ancients and crafted by our love's embrace.

Our life force shrivels to almost nothing.
Our despair which has been parted at bay
Has now risen to the depths of our city.

Our world now frozen in time and the only thing
I am good for right now is to comfort the last remaining
Piece of our life. Tears which have not escaped my cheeks

In years, are in hope to shed for you now,
As I shall walk the path to calm our city to calm you.
You, my everything. The softened kiss of my cracked lips,

Your smile spread wide, cheek to cheek,
Your heavenly eyes sparkle.
When Venus looks down her cheeks blushed.

Every person, celestial, Gods, were jealous
Of your empyrean beauty.

Spreading upon your forehead as you huddle the fire
For warmth to cover your body, since it now is covered
By those of colden memories, now turning to glass

As our mirrors finish cracking. This world we have made
Is almost in tandem and each step I take my feet freeze
To the ground. I walk as fast as I can while being molted in place.

I cry out for all those who can hear me, yet everyone's
Ears are shut to the hospitality of their homes,
Protecting what they can, to escape being obliterated.

This makes my job harder on getting to them,
To make them listen. The pass of tears breaking each
Part of me in ruins until my body collapses and the dream

World has now overtaken my every movement.

The atrcities I have seen when my eyes, awke;
Seeing they have prmised me 'f a warmth and pckets full
'f nothing, but the articulate, sft blades of grass
Which praises the entire land. Cnversations between
Myself start to apprach in the distance as this land is

Unknwn. This wrld, the arguments between him, I, brke
Thru t' 'nly an understatement I can see nw, which has a tll.
I peer in clser and all I see is this wrld mving faster
Then the 'ne I have left frm. The sun seemingly runs free
And 'nly retaining thse wh have cme this far and yet, his

Wrds are mine? I cannt remember this dream. Is this a past
Memry? Sustaining all these righteus mments. My eg 'n blast
Frgetting all these blissful times in a wrld dead to sustain
The medicrity I have created. Glry we made and share is a glimpse 'f fame

We have 'urselves, when making a wrld where the Gds were us, and
Nbdy else culd be 'r even have any pwer. My eyes glance away frm myself
Arguing with myself and as my head shifts, there yu are, the day I met yu.
The dress that decrates yur bdy hasn't changed, even in my mind.
The cmplexities we added and here is the mst simplest mment.

This is where peace has flurished in my bdy. My bdy banded
And I cannt lk away frm yur beauty. Hitting my purest self,

105

I nw see what true equity we sught t'reach. My spirit flew

Abve me, reminding me, everything is meant fr a higher purpse, yet I cannt sign

This saying t'give up 'n yu. I will nt ever let yu ut 'f my arms. I have bent

Befre and I will nt break. I will nt lse yu after centuries.

My heart shatters and breaks fr I have failed us in 'ur endeavrs and buried

My sul and 'ver stuffed my feelings; trying t'bear it all and nw, lk at me.

I am brken in half and this happy dream nw has a salty aftertaste leaving be,

The dark and deslate being 'f my wake. I can feel my insides quake

As my lve fr yu grws and starts t'quiver in my presence 'f failure.

My chest 'verfilled with emtins I cannt cntrl. This nightmare is all

Because 'f me. Hw srry I am t'yu, my lve. Making this perfect wrld

And nw I realize I can n'lnger cntinue t'rule in this made up wrld.

All I can think is hw nw I can n'lnger await my ultimate being and remake

'Ur perfectin with 'ur wrlds and the beings I made fr yu which is nw sub-dued the liar

Prspect I created. Heart shattered t'what I believed t'be true reality. Jur-nals I dreamt tame the ones I found. We were falling

Thru this true reality which I hid thru these mirr'r verses. The rainbws stretched

Acrss the universes we ruled until they landed upn us. Brken and freezing. My stench

'F failure lights the sky. 'Ur city nw ruled by the chas we tk away. Dminat-ing every

Aspect 'f my lve t'yu. Nw yu which I will and have always treasure

Is decaying and I cannt pass this wretched garden. My bdy starts t'fade in

And 'ut and I nw see the ruin clearly. My bdy frzen in time and I start t'
cnditin

My legs back and furth, desperately trying t'get t'yu. This miraculus
dream

Nw discntinued and reality back 'n track. I cry out and the beam

Of my voice could not reach the people.

My legs freezing in time and my love, built on a sanctioned steeple,

Is the only thing getting me through.

Our love elegantly aligned and shining through to the delicate destined truth.

My voice can only give one last boom

And bright light raised my Godly voice, the words took power and zoomed

Throughout our world, the people were

Calmed. A tear of humility has escaped my eyes and only for

You I shall elect to be vulnerable with.

I love you in eternal destiny's bliss.

As my feet tear off from the ground

Buried by snow, I turn back to our house to unbound

My beautiful flower. My love's inspiration

For these people echo on to my great love for her and the deprivation

I have always had in my heart towards

107

These weird creatures. My stride getting longer and I am now running forward

To my love in hope she is okay from saving
The people's voices for her. I run faster all while trying to tame

My mind. I am almost to the door.
And as I got through the door I tore

It open. I rushed inside, calling out to you.
As I turned the corner I saw you, your heart soared

From the ground. Shattered glass
Turned to sand. My heart deteriorated fast

As I see your lifeforce drained
From your being. I saved you and yet your last heartbeat rained

From your soul. My being raped
Of its joy and pleasure. I am completely kept

In shadows and drained of importance.
I am emptied on my power and love and since

I have been loving you for years
And never felt such despair; I fear

I will never get through this
Heartache. We ached for love after our last kiss

And I couldn't redo anything
We have missed since. My bones tighten

In despair. My love I
Miss you. You haven't been gone for long, but the sight

Of your love is already gone.
The remainder of the glass is less than a ton,

Weighing nothing, thrusted into
My chest. As she takes her last breathe, my sweet flew

Of a song which barely leaves my lips.
My love gone, my breath gone, departed upon my lips.

Annoyances string together lasting depths
Of new voyages that are all stringed together

In our paths chosen by our love for each other.
We started in ancient Egypt, when they fell,

We turned to Greece. We studied with the great
Philosophers of Europe and Persia before meeting

The great Achilles and traveling the seas to
The land of Gods where we learned to turn our

Temporary life to a very permanent life full of
Love and adventure. Again slipped the thought of making

Our own universes by the mirrors.
Love, you're my only delicate philosopher.

You are my only one, I truly love.
I would study the cosmos for you.

I will make you our own universe where we are Gods.
Knowledge is everything in this world,

If I can possess it all, we can rule the universes;
Ours and this one. Your heart's wishes are what will be true.

"'When she is on the mountain high,
By day, and in the silent night,
When all the stars shown clear and bright,
That I have heard her cry,
'Oh misery! Oh misery!
Oh woe is me! Oh misery!'"
For she in desolate sight
The most beautiful that night.
Nothing shown nearly as bright.
Clear as night and day, on the mountain top high,
She cried loud and high as her love poured to me that night.

Part Four:
Our Missing Writings
To Her: Our Journals of
the Old World

As these people scrounge through our things
Only one thing across the universe was found.
My letters are full of my love to you. The recreations
Of the world's most gifted writers. Entailed to
You below, I never showed them to you.
They were going to be a gift, given after your
Disease was cured.

The Thorn, a sad story about love and continuity between a despaired child forever gone in a world too cold and cruel to a loving mother. This is my recreation for you.

I.

There is a woman. She looks so young.

How could anyone disagree?—with your beauty—

Has she ever been born?

She is so brilliant and brave,

Yet older in soul than any man of age.

She rises high. Aged soul stands tall.

She is perfect in every meaning. No rough edges.

She is in a mass depression turned to loving happiness.

She is no longer forlorn.

Standing tall she asserts like a stone,

Endangering her timid heart she encased it again.

II.

And again uncased through all but one.

She enters a mass of catastrophe.

Her melancholy soul creeps to open once again.

Yes, old in wisdom, beauty young and although

This may seep; she runs

Creating her own control.

She did her best to lock the case forever,

But feelings are endeavors we cannot escape.

She threw them away and buried it moreover

Until one day she was taken by surprise

And guided throughout the night. This was Fate.

III.

Her soul stands as an Egyptian Queen.

Everything starts off as a fainted conversation

Which turns out to be deep and poetical.

Full of knowledge and instincts.

As the darkness slowly comes over this world, a beam

Of light with no limitations.

How can we turn a life into fellowship?

Love on verge, at the peak, on brink,

To the fully open life of love you're promised.

Your eyes are still young as the meteor shower passes by.

Yet as you speak, wisdom still seeps.

IV.

"Fate takes our lives as a simulation.

Always reaching for greatness.

I am always going for the best sitting contemplating.

No matter what it is, anyone can test this.

My soul looking for someone who also is.

Always extending to do everything.

Someone as ambitious as I am.

I know it's scary to accomplish, but you have a list.

Allow those feeling to be uncased from the ground,

To forever follow where you need to go; instead bounding

Yourself with all of the other weak minds."

V.

Oh your beauty shines through as those star

Constellations fly across your eyes.

Sunglasses cover your eyes as you leave no byes.

Leather coat shines like diamonds

Splitting the walkways. A queens radar

Is different from all others. Like mine.

Today's world, our confidence can get us in a bind.

Yet, you and I have no conditions.

Your heart conquers the world

And anyone who has heard,

Know your the meaning in everyone's world.

VI.

It would be different if you were just smart.

Except you're not.

Your beautiful, intelligent, strong-willed,

Deep lover, force to be reckoned with,

Independent, sparkle, light up every room,

Go-getter, passionate, charismatic,

Visionary, dreamer, truth-teller,

Decision-maker, eyes that make anyone crazy,

Hard worker, determined, personality, joyous,

Devoted, whole hearted, inspiring,

Mesmerizing, immaculate, sensational, inspirational; just to name a couple.

VII.

Every day and night this sensational woman

Creates beauty every day.

The longing each day pertains to my

Contained soul awaiting for our reunion.

Oh how I wait for the day

To be in your grasp once again. Until then, I sigh.

Oh how my heart awaits for the revolution

Til hands meet hands and arms meet arms;

Oh what a gracious moment indeed.

I shall forever contaminate my thorns
Which shall never stab such love, believe.

VIII.

As all the seasons change
A presence seeps to be.
I maintain the trouble to get to know you
And yet you see, I somehow think we're meant to be.
Why is this woefoe thought upon me?
I dream of something more, something bigger
And yet it seems you like something silver
And not this golden dream in my head.
Here I am and the woeful in me. Laying in bed
Searching for an understanding
Bringing us closer since never advancing.

IX.

What if by the time this was published
You saw it and I asked you to marry me?
Would you say yes? Would you call
Me a weirdo freak? Oh how glamorous
Is such a life. I should just wonder the city
To seek you every chance I get.
You would never say no. True rubbish.
Yes would be the truest answer. I saw
Such possibility. Desirability. Naturally
Drawn into ancient civilizations. Gritty
Souls drawn to one another with no conflict.

X.

In my dreams I've died
Next to your heart
In your arms.
Do I wander in your blessed dreams?
Oh, what shall cease my heart?
The pain of stinging chest collapses in.
Tyranny sits in, locking myself in a bind.
Should we always be destined to be apart?
Feels like solar systems are between us.
If the stars fell from the sky I'd stop
Everything, eternally, but they don't fall, do they?

XI.

Will your smile fade today?
I know today might not be so easy,
But darling, you must know
We got to conquer the world.
So girl, do you wish you were here?
Do you wish you were alive or dead?
Are you there? Are you in my head?
I understand life after death.
You die throughout life and you have
To know no matter even after you bathe
You're still dirty in a way.

XII.

What's the point of living if
We don't live for peace.
Excitement and calming
She carries me to my earthly nature.

The somber tone aches in the heartland.

I shall carry you further lifting

You high in the air. Releasing

The tension of the negligence bombing

You do to my ever tender heart.

Run to me and live life's awe.

For I shall carry you forever.

XIII.

Desperate glances at your intelligence.

Mercy! Oh mercy me! Such brilliance

Dangles in front of me.

That silky skin shines in the milky night.

Oh I hope the heavens truly see

This beautiful angel in earthly sight.

Take my hands tonight.

Deep melancholy strikes the mind of a silly boy,

But he now turns into a man scared of all

The imperfections he carried. He was coy

And thought no one could compare to you.

XIV.

Attached, she reached for his hands.

Softly, she relaxes them, pressed close

To his chest. Together they were banded

And the true gentleman does not boast

About anything, including the gentle softness of his woman.

Carefully and folded he pulled her close

And the woman blushed slightly for

She does not know what to think.

He promised to never bore

Her. On the brink
She is his world.

XV.

Only she could maintain her menacing
Beauty, for no one can compare.
Every day she is penciled
In his mind. He is no longer immature,
Carefully taking her in with him.
Oh Lord. Help him. He is in love.
Oh what a woman's love does to a man.
Her love, his love, what a contraption.
It is nothing like today's interaction.
He was an old lover with flowers and dinner.
After he took her to a movie..

XVI.

Fate has brought them together
As the author is detached from them.
Now all you see is the dreams
And rivers that pass through her beauty.
Like the sands of Egypt being embarked
On by the immaculate sculptures and pyramids.
Oh how the rainforests echo from her voice
When she sings the beautiful enchantment of the sea.
Oh faded memory, when I close my eyes I see
The distant relations of the grass themes, midwestern dreams.
Oh yes, everything you, she's true gold, even the words she speaks.

XVII.

Trades far and forever pass my wretched eyes

And your significance has me striving for greatness.

King of the world as you by my side makes Queen.

God like testimonies peer sight from blind my

Loving goddess. Some say perfectionist unhumbled.

I say God and Goddess deeply in my soul

Humbles by hers. Tickets being taken and toles

Being issued by my heart to hers. Oh how the inspired

Are now bystanders. I don't understand where their

Eyes are blinded by their own hate. Not her and that I love.

The love that saved us and perplexed us to greatness.

XVIII.

I see her again and my heart sings to me.

Oh how fate has brought us back together.

There is nothing more I love to see

Then my love in the early morning's breeze.

She is alive so are you awake yet?

The story begins as soon as the mother wakes.

She comes in and all is awake as she

Makes all human beings.

She doesn't see this though,

But every living being breathes life once again.

People look up to her and of course they now see.

XIX.

What do the people mean to her though?

I know she does not know her importance

In this perfection of a world she created.

Every day we continue to row

Down the stream in this forever dream.
Our love and fate are of sure certain,
I confidently believe you know it true.
This epic love story seeks to forever be.
Oh how my peers, the other gods, know
My heart is true to be. Oh powerful friends,
In the heavens, strike me down if this is untrue.

XX.

I have heard they gave me their approval
Because I know I am as alive as ever.
My peers have not yet struck me down.
No God has yet to do so even as I sit here,
Missing you forever, pondering if your
Still responding. Patience is slipping away as
I grasp the world for the patience I try to keep.
Oh, love please hurry back to me.
The soft loving manor of her eyes just looking at me;
And oh, how I appreciate just this sudden glance
To me. For just the attention gives my heart a pleasurable grasp.

XXI.

I hear them swear to me that she is
Not just exceptional to me.
Oh I wish she knew she was loved
And I wish she knew my love was pure
As can be. Oh her beauty, what if she knew.
A model would be born. The fashion
Goddess of beauty. My love
Succeeding everywhere around me.
Oh my love would be the most gorgeous

To walk this planet. If it was cold she would

Be in that oh maleficent jacket.

XXII.

"When she is on the mountain high,

By day, and in the silent night,

When all the stars shown clear and bright,

That I have heard her cry,

'Oh misery! Oh misery!

Oh woe is me! Oh misery!'"

For she in desolate sight

The most beautiful that night.

Nothing shown nearly as bright.

Clear as night and day, on the mountain top high,

She cried loud and high as her love poured to me that night.

As from the great William Wordsworth's, *The Thorn,*
Recreated for her blessed soul.
What more do you want me to prove?
Are you okay with it now?
Is society now welcoming of our quick, fast love?
Loosely phrased for maybe it's not.
I cannot for sure say at this point,
But oh, does my soul rejoice for hers.

Or how about the recreation of the
All mighty William Butler Yeats's, *When You Are Old?*

When my newly founded love and her brightly
Shown grace turns and fades away, as wrinkles
Show upon her olden face, I shall look at you
Deeply and tell you, oh how much I love you.

I shall turn to you and open your door politely
Smiling, seeing the slight blush as your eyes twinkle
At the kindness of mine. Even if you fall through
Into my arms I will look to

Help you up as I will always carry you in my arms.
Your eyes shall glisten and it will continue to charm
Me even in my olden ways. Our souls combine
Even into our last words which will softly rhyme.

As love has been gifted for more than me to you and we must share these desires completely at bare with him watching our every moment. We get through these hardships with him by the small communications between our solemn heart and enduring love we will always share. The great William Shakespeare has started this engraving to put our love on pedestals; but you, you should be a God who rules alongside of him in this ever expanding world.

If love is painful, then how can our minds
Admit hardships during forever marriage?
When is love a forever truth which isolates
Every meaning or removes every pen mark.
Eraser moves and the mark taints the board
The tainted line stretches continuously on
It's never shaken occurrence on the board.
Time is never Love's fool; lasting endlessly
Within the bullet under thumb, in it's gun.
Love's cheeks blushed and red upon lips
The stern kiss grasped for time's grasp.
Eagerness stern, edge of doom yearns
And if error be stings my words, conscious,
Never did I write, Never did man love.

Oh, how the creation of this dominate poem
Longed for recreation into this newer
Century. This centered on forever
Grace and my own dependity of life.
Oh how mighty one sixteen have
Raged the seas beneath.

Mighty Shakespeare reinvented poetry
To what we read and recognize as the early
Great of all time and I shall pave the

Way and go down in history as the greatest.
This love epic contains everything
Anyone would ever need to celebrate
Life with everyone in their life.

It is like when people claim to be
Wise and it is true they clearly
Do not know. Seas of knowledge
Hit us at once and yet we truly
Don't understand our past or future.
Nobody around me knows anything
About this gift I so desperately bring.
Shakespeare paved paths for
Everyone who has come after.
People who've embarked on
Such a wild journey of love and peace.

The reason I mentioned wise and wind
Is because one author who considered
Not one of the greatest should be up there.
Christina Rossitti. Oh, those mid eighteen hundreds.
A creation of such bliss is needed
For she is yet another poet who has soared
Rightfully to the top and one I must
Head to and give proper celebration.
"I loved you first:But afterwards your love"

Oh, how I cannot weigh our
Love on a scale of who loves who the most
For it is not love, that is weighed and it
Is for love, that we cannot hold down by

Such human measures. The path of the right
Love's only sought by those who seek, not boast
About such beautiful measures. Conflict
Is that we must aim to not achieve because
Your love outshined mine, though I loved you
Before you loved me. Oh, even now, a new
Concept to most of those who do love.
Because again no chains weighs down the dove
Like feelings. Soaring high anywhere
Because love is forever eternally.
How I miss the butterflies
Which fluttered aimlessly through my stomach.
Oh, Miss. Rossitti, such perfection
In your poetry.

Just like the historic John Keats: *When I have fears that I may cease to be*
My love for you is standing here on the great shores,
While my mind and soul debate back and forth

On whether I should tell you.
My soul wants nothing more than to be with you.
Oh delicate old soul I hope you win out.

My mind, tells a different story
Of betrayal and disloyalty.
Oh beauty condemned my head and intelligence

Allowing my soul to power through this bleak moment
Of injustice my mind is putting me through.
Oh, how I could end up loving you.

Or how about the great Edgar Allen Poe.
Annabel Lee, a great love story
With such tragedy.

Many years have past, long ago
In a kingdom further away by the sea,
Oh, my gorgeous love lives there; you may know
Her by the name of Frey;
She was so brilliant in her own way.
To be loved and worship by life's own desired glee.

As she was young, I was young,
In this place far by the sea.
But we loved with a love, bigger than love
My Frey to be.
This love was with from Seraphs heaven
That conveyed my love, the mighty Frey.

Here it was, long ago
A wind chilled my love
In that kingdom by the sea.
Oh, our warmth has faded
And the death betrayed
Taken by Angels wings.
The feelings I felt after this
Made me question if love is really hate.

All the angels were shocked with awe
At the death which befalleth her.
Envious they gathered and looked upon us
As the chill has killed my Frey;

Blowing its mighty winds toward me.
Her eyes, sad as the beauty is drained.

But our love is stronger more further
Than anyone older than we
Than anyone wiser than we
Than any other soul to be.
No angel; No demon,
Can never dissect my heart from
My beautiful Goddess Frey.

As stars rise, moons beam, I slumber in my dreams
Of my Goddess Frey.
I can see her brightly lit face, when those stars do rise
Of my Angel Frey.
As my side is laid on and the waters tide on mind
Until dreams take me to my love and bride,
My Frey forever taken to the sky,
My Frey forever ruling above in the sky.

These poets from the influential
Poetry era were not
Tortured artists, but they were
Artists in love with the people,
The land, and they trusted these
Beautiful souls. They are not these
Helpless, wretched, tortured artists we
As the new generation makes them out to be.
They were on their own journey's of life,
Like so many of us are currently.
Every new day poet hopes and dreams

To accomplish the popularity and the

Brilliance these poets acquired.

These poets were in utter love with their natures,

Their people, their societies.

How have we strayed so far from the path?

Epilogue:

The End.

Truth be told no one can adhere
To such velocity as you and yours truly.
What a true love story.

Even after everything, I sit here bottles
In, pondering if you would still care.
Even though my face numb,
Waiting for my head to clear
I ache for the days I was coddled
With love, I miss the days of fun.

Every time the music glitches
My head spins, but when it's on,
My mind relaxes and ditches
To where my mind cons

My soul into thinking the aching
Of such hidden garden makes
Me hide in detest, as your love
Aches to be mine; so sing does the dove

As I recreate these masterful pieces
All in your name to try and impress you,
As the blade enters my breast plate.

I want to be persistent;
But someday you and I will no longer be
Of this world. Whatever we see fit the business
We had will leave and ultimately bleed for we

Never conspired with each other.

How can I judge what you do,
Being alive and maneuvering I know

I have failed because it reentered my
Blood stream and an old conversation
Comes flooding back to me.

Sometimes I want to live, never again,
And in your somber, beautiful eyes,
I can tell you feel the same, as I sigh.

Oh pure thought, reenter my mind
As love leaves to keep you in my mind.
This drunken state deems service

In this hollow being of a man.
You glue me together and yet
After all these years you're the one they bet

To tear me apart after such talent.
They say I am not intact
And yet they call me illiterate.

Pureness you bring makes me brilliant.
What a dreadful day,
How can you not say
Different, because now it seems like it's all in my head.

Imaginary and undisciplined,
Lessons regarded in natural glisten
To sustain our love sick obsessions.

Is mine the only in this despaired cycle?
Banished sentencing of a failed
Stench of not asking you sooner

To be questioning myself now
After you no longer appear
In my everyday sight.

My head as a king to queen bows
At your every movement. Being a seer,
Watching your future with me unwind tonight.

Dreams march in the fields of my heart
Desperate for us never to part.
Longing my mind for what I thought was a solution

Too many issues in past aggressions.
Oh my dear syringa, all is well,
Might be a feasible possession.

I just see one day soon
Like a caterpillar sprouting from a cocoon
Twisting into a feeble bell.

Life underwhelming and in spirits delight
Nobody has tempted me in the dim light, night.
If daylight brings beauty, darkness needs an understanding.

If there was a perfect person waiting,
You would be her. Rumors containing

As one turns to two.

Looking upon my hands, blood
Appearing in a blink and the second
Turned back to one. All our memories flooding

To me, circling as I flew
My way in my dreams.
I wish you were here so we could talk.
Maybe one day I can overlook this strife.

It's nobody's fault my jealousy
Is too intact. I wish freelancing was
My way. Completely desolate, yet enchanting.

Anguish and proximity lay this peaceful
Feeling surrounding me because
Everything has happened since your office, feasibly

Aching in painful remorse.
I recreate these masterpieces for your love;
Beauty of everlasting butterflies circle like a dove.

I ache for these to reach you, coming fourth
Until these doves can finally leave when I hear your name.
You and I can reach such heights, and our fame

Will echo throughout the never ending halls
Of Valhalla and God's lasting garden.
We would make angels cry as they fly

Overhead, trying to make sure certain

Beings bow to the presence we make.

Just like the clash of the titans contemplating

Where we can share our imperfections

As desolate shapes turn them into worshiping points.

These beings have no privacy or contemptions.

Oh how desperate I feel to ever seek your attention,

So bleak my attempts must strike you.

Oh here I go again, but yet your radiance

Is too high to be measured in capacity.

No one has ever shown such elegance.

Sparks and flames shower ahead

Deep in the night sky, apprehending the trance

You so undoubtedly put me in.

Oh I never knew poetry until now.

When you enter my mind and just like poetry I take a bow.

For the true art in front of me

Allowing my eyes and mind take form

Of the delicacy I am tormented with.

Oh what strange feelings it takes

To keep up distant and yet, unlike

Modern day, I continue to forsake

My own frozen heart which cannot be warmed

During these chilled Iceland days
Without you by my side. I may not stand

And dance, the fool I am, in circles
When your presence is nigh.
Oh your presence so dreamy

As my craft in such golden divinity.
Every time mind drifts to your
Milky skin, soft in touch,

Breathes, contemplating for
Such love and respect embarks trust
Within frequency.

My heart pounds, even now,
Echoing back to a time reflections
Were shown to you through mirrors

Reflecting through clothing.
As I start to think about these mirrors
I start to recall creation and making universes.

How my knowledge can grow to make you your own.
Just like now though, when I reach out to you,
My heart thuds when my phone makes a buzz,

I look down and yet your name is never the one
Who is seen while I continuously pursue
Where my heart is no longer being wanted.

Yet, it is I who knows this and still yearns for your words
To spill across my phone screen, just like a letter back
In the eighteenth century.

It is funny how we came this far.
We used to get letters that truly meant something,
Now we get texts from strangers saying I love you which means nothing.

No matter how many times
Any words come across my screen,

Every thought that spills my mind,
Runs longer and longer,
Yet it is here, where these words,

Are picked carefully and in no bind;
As those misguided prints be as those who've mugged
Me and my words intensively. Your image is burned

Inside my mind, yet blurred in my thoughts
About mysterious daggers who plagued my gratitude, to you.
I've fallen in love with someone who doesn't remember

What it was like to see me every day.
To speak hours on end, though, few,
I believe would have happened frequently

If we weren't scared of our emotions, intensity.

Splendor, joy, and passion press
Through despite agony of once cherished

Personal emotion we once carried.

My hearts' glamor goes out to a soul, none
Other than yourself. We were at our best
When we completely dove

Into our deep, intellectual, conversation.
Not all the time though, when we discussed
Old movies and sad melancholy we each digested

Moving on towards happier thoughts.
They were carried by your smile which
Never grew bigger when we were talking through and through.
Even now, after these months, alone,
I still wish you were here, because the ache
Of being alone, without you, is painful.

These other people, they don't get me like you
And some of them really try and they want to;
I don't necessarily think they need to though.

What if you come back here?
What if you start to answer again?
What if...What if...What if...

This goes through my mind now when I hear
A resemblance of your so blessed name which makes
Me want to write in the old language that intoxicates us.

All I can think is how to
Continuously subdue

Thoughts to not mimic you

As I try to continue on.
Although I am not stuck
However, I do wish your name

Wouldn't take me back to those
Leather boots, leather coat,
Black hair, dark eyes, and milky skin.

Oh, how when I saw you today
I just wanted to tell you how beautiful
You looked, but again I stuttered.

How I wish I could be in your elegance
So I may not look a fool when I speak to you.
I can't wait until our next chat.

I just need to find you again. See your beauty glisten.
Take you to dinner. We can articulate and we can depend.
We can see the world. See those eyes glimmer.

I have failed in the exquisite duties of my life
As I have said I never would, and yet, I am here,
The failed presence I entered into my psychology.

Shy as can be intelligence seeping,
As a fractured desolate beauty.
Hanging onto the slight hope of a lost respect

Founded by each other into the deep abyss

You might not even exist.
A scared child I was and hid from problems reality shaped.

Echoed into existence the middle crush of life
Was darker than anyone meant to me.
Hid again from another crush I wished you

Shined alongside the courageous life your
Maturity always showed you to be.
Slightly angled to the rainbow decorated into existence

By your penetrating anguish.
Sweet desires and pleasantry delight
Fashion into a sunsets bliss of mastered color.

What makes you special?
I gave her a piece of mine, will she return in favor?
What if my fear for a healthy relationship condemns me of self sabotage?
What if I had a child somewhere in the world and I have always been too scared to figure it out?
What if my fears and flaws are too large?
What if I do not add up to the man I want to be?
What if I do not add up to your expectations?

Past relationships nail at the back of my mind
And yet, you're the only thing circulating my mind.
I miss your company and your presence my lady.

My Queen, lady, woman, I miss you with every
Calm beat of my heart. My forever queen, lay your head
Softly onto my chest and drift away peacefully.

My heart has gone down the wrong path
Too many times, but you are the right one
I know it. The trinity of my being

Says it all. Dreams of you never stop.
My vulnerability for you is something I
Cherish and I know right now we are not to the stage
Of complete disciplined, heart wrenching, obsessed
Lovers we were meant to be.

If I continue to feel discarded and worthless
Will you make me feel good enough?
This doubt stales my mind, making me
Paralyzed as the death planted into me
Sterilizes my being and makes me ill,
Yet this doubt still carries all the weight.

Is fine, but is it for you? What if I don't strongly believe
In one thing or another. What if they aren't even real?
Would you still love me if you knew everything about me?

What if I released my dream journal about us.
Are you okay with my mess?